Ormond Beach Historic Places

A Guide to Walk, Bike and Drive Our History

Ronald L. Howell

and

Alice R. Howell

Ormond Beach Historic Places

A Guide to Walk, Bike and Drive Our History

Printed in the United States of America. All rights reserved under International Copyright Law. Contents and/or cover may not be reproduced or transmitted in whole or in part in any form or by any means without the express written consent and permission of the authors, Ronald L. and Alice R. Howell

Copyright 2007 – Ronald L. and Alice R. Howell

Ormond Beach Historic Places

ISBN 978-1-4243-3089-8

Halifax Country Publisher
P O Box 4088
Ormond Beach, FL 32175-4088

Printed January 15, 2007 by: Dolphin Printing and Design Inc.
                                2334 E. Highway 100 Suite 7E
                                Bunnell, Fl 32110

Additional copies of the book may be obtained via:

www.halifaxcountry.com

You may also send additional book request orders to:

Halifax Country Publisher
P O Box 4088
Ormond Beach, FL 32175-4088

A Guide to Walk, Bike and Drive Our History

Preface

Ormond Beach Historic Places provides a detailed, accurate and interesting presentation of Ormond Beach history plus a mapped guide to walk, bike, and drive our local history. In other words, this book is a self guide to locate and visit Ormond Beach historic places.

The introduction provides an understanding of the political, economic and environmental factors influencing Ormond's growth and development as conquerors and pioneers alike struggled to cultivate and settle Halifax Country.

The traveler portion of the book provides driving directions and maps to the sites, information about Ormond's historic sites, and current pictures of what has been preserved today. Our goal as authors is to bring the history of these most important historical places in line with the stories and facts associated with present day Ormond Beach.

A detailed timeline provides a chronological order to historical events surrounding our important Ormond Beach history. Like life's journey, there is a beginning, a middle and end.

Ormond's historic beginning has a very long prehistoric period beginning approximately 20,000 years ago and ending somewhere around the 1500's.

Our middle history involves exploration and occupation by several countries and the decline in our primitive Indian civilizations. The 1600's marked a time of great change for the native people and landscape of North America. European colonists began to arrive on the shores of this great and mysterious land, but, unlike earlier explorers and traders, these white strangers were looking for a place to live. The French, English and Dutch landed on the northeast shores while the Spanish and English established themselves in the south.

The end, as you may have guessed, is our future. We are living the end because we understand our recent history up to today. History changes each and every day and will continue to change as we preserve our past, while living our future.

Please help keep history alive as we journey forward, remembering those who came before us and struggled to make this a better place to live, work, raise families and make history.

Dedication

Alice and I dedicate this book to all those who came before us and sacrificed so much, as Ormond Beach grew out of a very hostile and extremely difficult environment. We can only begin to understand the sacrifices made by our courageous forefathers, but we can take a few moments and thank each and every individual that stayed the course and paved the way for the rest of us.

Many lives were lost along the way. People endured hardships greater than we can imagine and individual accomplishments prevailed. We thank our forefathers for making Ormond Beach a most wonderful place to live and raise our families.

We also want to thank our families and friends for their support, enthusiasm, suggestions and encouragement as we researched, wrote and published our second book. Thanks to you all.

Our special heartfelt thanks is again extended to Don Bostrom (Historian Emeritus) for his inspiration and encouragement throughout this process. Our first book "Our Place in History – Ormond Beach, Florida" was dedicated to J. Donald Bostrom, grandson of John Andrew Bostrom (first settler on the peninsula) , and we are equally proud to share our second dream come true with Don. We truly felt the love, respect and admiration of Don and his grandfather, for each other and Ormond, as we researched and published this book. Thanks Don, our cherished friend.

A Guide to Walk, Bike and Drive Our History

Table of Contents

Preface
Dedication
Introduction

Table of Contents

Description	Page
Silver Bluff Terrace	1
Timucuan Indians	2
Nocoroco	3
Spanish Establish First Permanent Residence in Florida	4
Spain Ceded Florida to the British	5
King's Road (Florida's First Highway)	5
British Disband Florida	6
Captain James Ormond I	6
The Territorial Period	8
Live Oakers Play an Important Role	9
Earliest Pioneers – Ormond Peninsula	10
First Florida Retirement Community is Born	11
Isolation Continues Until Railroad Arrives	13
The Hotel Ormond is Built	14

Ormond Beach Historic Places

Henry Morrison Flagler Returns to St Augustine .	15
Henry Flagler's Influence is Great News	15
A Time of Growth	16
Ormond Beach, the "Birthplace of Speed" is Born	18
John D. Rockefeller Comes to Town	18
Wintering in Florida Declines	20
The Good News is Presented in the Pages of this Book	21
Map – Ormond Beach NE Quadrant	22
Map – Ormond Beach SE Quadrant	23
Map – Ormond Beach NW Quadrant	24
Map – Ormond Beach SW Quadrant	25
The Casements	26
Fortunato Park and the Hotel Ormond Cupola	28
Talahloka	30
Trappers Lodge	32
71 Orchard Lane	34
Nathan Cobb Cottage	36
Ormond Garage	38
The Birthplace of Speed Park	40
Nathan Cobb Shipwreck	42
Memorial Art Museum and Gardens	46
Emmons Cottage	48

A Guide to Walk, Bike and Drive Our History

Billy's Tap Room & Grill	50
MacDonald House	52
Riverway	54
Bosarve	56
Lion House	58
McSwain House LaTourette (Little Tower)	60
Rowallan/Lisnaroe	62
Hammock Home	64
Number 9 Plantation	66
Bulow Plantation Ruins	68
Fairchild Oak	70
Tomb of James Ormond II	72
Dummett Plantation Ruins	74
Nocoroco and Tomoka Basin	76
Dix House	78
William McNary Home	80
Ormond Yacht Club	82
Anderson-Price Memorial Library (Village Improvement Association and (Woman's Club)	84
James Carnell Home	86
Pilgrim's Rest Primitive Baptist Church	88
Lippincott Mansion (Melrose Hall)	90

The Porches	92
"The Whim" at Ames Park and Ames House	94
Ormond Indian Mound	96
Rigby School	98
Ormond Elementary School	100
The Three Chimneys	102
Halifax Country Timeline	105
A Brief Bibliography of Florida History	117
Our Place in History – Front Cover	120
Our Place in History – Rear Cover	121
About the Authors	123

A Guide to Walk, Bike and Drive Our History

Introduction

Silver Bluff Terrace

Ormond Beach is located on the Silver Bluff Terrace, an ancient ocean bottom that was formed during the last Glacial Period – approximately 20,000 years ago. Ground sloths (shown below), rearing approximately twelve feet high, once roamed our forests along-side saber-toothed tigers, mammoths, mastodons, giant armadillos, camels, prehistoric horses and the like.

Twelve thousand years ago the first man came to Florida. These descendants of primitive Asiatics who migrated over the land bridge came to be called Indians. They hunted the animals along the Halifax and Tomoka Rivers, planted crops and fished the rivers, leaving shell mounds and middens behind.

These mounds indicate that their makers ate, among other things, oysters and clams. Broken pottery, arrowheads, spear points and other artifacts have been found in abundance. At the time these people inhabited the area, the Halifax River would have been a shallow, fresh-water stream. One of the early burial mounds has been preserved and is described later in this book.

Timucuan Indians

The Timucuan Indians made this area their home in the early 1500's. The Timucuan Tribe was one of six main tribes occupying Florida when the Spaniards made their first visit. The local tribes lived in fortified villages along the Tomoka and Halifax Rivers. What we know of them comes, in part, from the detailed diaries and drawings of the French explorer Jacques LeMoyne. He wrote of tawny, muscular people who were accomplished craftsmen in many ways. They were experts in weaponry, clay pottery, jewelry, and clothing, made mostly of deerskin and moss.

Physical fitness was a prized attribute of the Timucuan people. Training sessions in the form of "games" were common tribal activities. They were also excellent fishermen, hunters, and warriors.

Since they lived near the coast, their food consisted mainly of fish and vegetables grown in their small farms along the river shores. In the winter, they moved to warmer inland forests where they ate the berries, nuts, and herbs that grew wild.

A Guide to Walk, Bike and Drive Our History

Nocoroco

The primary settlement was called "Nocoroco" and was mapped by the Spanish in 1602 showing its location where Tomoka State Park is today.

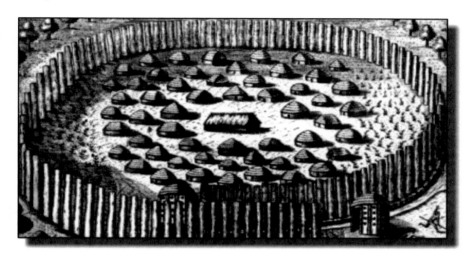

A Timucuan Village Sketch, circa 1564.

Spanish captain DePrado documented this village in late 1569 in writings to the King of Spain. DePrado also documented the declining welfare of this tribe. In the early 1600's, Alvaro Mexia was sent on exploring expeditions down Florida's northeast coast and in 1602 created a map, which shows Nocoroco on a peninsula between two rivers. This is thought to be at the convergence of Tomoka River and what is now the Halifax River. The Halifax River is actually an estuary which is a water passage where the ocean tide meets a river current.

The Tomoka, a corruption of the Indian word Timucua, was named during the British period. The Halifax River was later named after the President of the Board of Trade, George Montagu Dunk, the Earl of Halifax.

Within 200 years after DePrado's expedition, the Timucuans entirely disappeared from the east coast of Florida. It is thought their susceptibility to diseases brought by the Spaniards, raids from the Yamassee Indians, and the British raids from North Carolina sped their demise.

Farther south were other Indian villages along the Halifax. Two of these, Caracoy and Cicale, were located along the west side of the Halifax River in or near the present city limits of Ormond Beach. One of these villages is thought to be associated with the Ormond Mound, located just south of the Ormond Beach city hall.

Spanish Establish First Permanent Residence in Florida

The Spanish were the first Europeans to establish a permanent presence in Florida. This was called The First Spanish Period and they ruled Florida from 1565 to 1763. During this period the Spanish never really established a densely populated or intensely developed area. St Augustine, the principle Spanish settlement, served as a military outpost and a point of departure for missionaries seeking to Christianize Indians living in outlining areas.

The first Spanish governor, Pedro Menendez, attempted to establish colonial agricultural settlements thus providing livestock and foodstuffs on their ranches (missions). Missions were established throughout central and eastern Florida and as far north as the Carolinas.

The Spanish method of gathering the indigenous Florida Indians into mission centers to convert them into their culture greatly contributed to their extinction, by the early 1700's. Once gathered into densely populated missions, they lost their customary methods of survival and became vulnerable to epidemics. In a desperate effort to find Indian allies, the Spanish encouraged the movement of Creeks into Florida to fill the void left by the devastated, indigenous Timucuans.

After 1763, the Spanish, with few exceptions, evacuated Spanish missions en masse. This departure opened the door for the new Florida governor, James Grant, to begin distribution of very large British land grants to his subjects. James Grant had ambitions to develop Florida as "Britannia's New Eden."

A Guide to Walk, Bike and Drive Our History

Spain Ceded Florida to the British

At the end of the Seven Years War in Europe (1756 – 1763), Spain ceded Florida to the British in exchange for Cuba. It was not until Florida became a British colony that pioneer settlers come to the area. The British government gave many massive land grants to its influential subjects, including 20,000 acres to well connected Richard Oswald in 1766. Mount Oswald was a rice and indigo plantation encompassing what is now Tomoka State Park. Indigo was big business during Oswald's time and was sent back to England for use as a dye for cloth and paints as well as a bluing agent for laundry. Naturalized indigo can still be found in the area today.

Kings Road (Florida's First Highway)

While under British occupation Florida's first highway, The Kings Road, was begun in 1771 and completed in 1775. It covered 106 miles from St. Augustine to New Smyrna Beach and 48 miles from Palatka to Amelia Island. This portion of the Kings Road (the Lost Causeway) was rediscovered in 1880 by John Anderson and Charles Bostrom.

British Disband Florida

When the British left in 1783, the meager beginnings of a plantation capital fell into ruin and did not flourish again until the Spanish land grants of the early 1800's brought planters from the Bahamas. When the Spanish reclaimed Florida, their world power had weakened considerably. Spain was faced with the dilemma of too few colonists, forcing it to give up its policy of requiring settlers to convert to Catholicism. This encouraged many English planters to return to Florida in the early 1800's. Generous land grants were awarded to well-placed Anglos willing to invest in developing Northeast Florida lands into productive plantations.

Spain continued to encourage Creek Indians to migrate into Florida. Creek Indians were more than willing to escape harsh U.S. policies. Runaway slaves also sought their freedom in the newly established Spanish colony. Many U.S. citizens considered Florida a sanctuary for enemies of the United States government. Land hungry settlers also considered Florida an easy target for territorial expansion. These factors eventually led to the notorious 1818 invasion of Spanish Florida by Andrew Jackson. Spain was in possession of Florida from 1783 to 1821, when it then became a United States Territory.

James and George Anderson, benefactors of the Spanish land grants, came to Ormond and settled an area that had been a British plantation of earlier times – Mount Oswald. The Dummett's had also settled in Ormond, taking the land grant that included Rosetta Plantation, former holding of the Moultrie family during British occupation.

Captain James Ormond I

North of the Anderson Plantation (Cobb's Corner) and the Dummett's Plantation was Damietta, the cotton and indigo plantation of the Ormond family. Captain James Ormond I received a 2,000-acre land grant for his Damietta Plantation. Ormond I was killed in 1817 by a runaway slave and the family moved back to Scotland.

A Guide to Walk, Bike and Drive Our History

James Ormond II returned to Damietta with his wife and four children, including James Ormond III in 1820. When James Ormond II died in 1829, his family abandoned Damietta. He is buried about four miles north of Tomoka State Park. James Ormond III would return many years later.

Little did he, or any other pioneers, foresee the hostilities about to come. The Second Seminole Indian War erupted in 1835. The battle was about hunting and fishing grounds and the freedom of movement of the Indians. There was a tremendous uprising against the planters and a massive evacuation to St. Augustine took place. The plantations fell victim to fiery raids.

"Bulow Ville," one of the most glamorous and wealthy of all the plantations, became a military outpost until the Indians came too close, too often. Soon Bulow Ville became a victim of the strife and only ruins remain today.

Bulow Ville, As It Exists Today.

Ormond Beach Historic Places

The Territorial Period

In the early 19th century, armed incursions across Spanish boundaries of Florida by the U.S. forces pursuing runaway slaves and Creek Indians created an undeclared invasion of Spanish Territory. Years of military challenges toward dwindling Spanish defenses lessened this already weak grip the Spanish government had on Florida. Spain had little choice but to cede Florida to the United States in 1821.

In spite of this change in Florida's ownership, Florida plantations continued to flourish. Plantation owners used the latest industrial and steam-powered technologies in its large-scale sugar production. All of this ended with the outbreak of the Second Seminole War in 1835.

During the winter of 1835 – 1836, the citizens of St Augustine watched in dismay as clouds of billowing smoke drifted towards the city from the south. Except for the slave quarters, the Seminole Indians burned all of the plantations along the Halifax and Tomoka Rivers to the ground. Efforts to save the plantations were futile. The people of St Augustine provided refuge for an exodus of plantation owners and workers. Within one month, the once thriving plantations from Pellicer Creek to Cape Canaveral were reduced to ruins.

Osceola, a Seminole warrior, provided leadership until he sickened late in 1837. This leadership was shared variously between Wildcat, Alligator, Jumper, Halleck, Billy Bowlegs and Sam Jones (Abiaka). The United States sent its top four generals against the Seminoles, and each left Florida with his reputation diminished.

One of the top generals, Major General Thomas S. Jesup, claiming treachery on the part of the Indians, began to capture their leaders any way he could. Most notorious was his seizure of Osceola under a flag of truce on 27 October 1837. Jesup also succeeded in splitting the black warriors away from the Seminoles. When the Second Seminole war ended in 1842, the sugar and cotton plantations along the Halifax and Tomoka Rivers were destroyed – never to be restored again.

A Guide to Walk, Bike and Drive Our History

Live Oakers Play An Important Role

From the 1840's until the early 1870's this area was primarily wilderness. Live oaks, in particular, were cut from the interior and transported to the coast where they were shipped for processing.

Tomoka Avenue in Ormond Beach was originally a live oak logging road, leading to the Halifax River. The Swift family (three brothers) from New England was the principal contractor in this area and had purchased the Oswald grant in 1850 for their logging business.

During the years before the Civil War, they produced several thousand board feet of live oak and other ship timber. Florida's live oak trees were used to build both military and commercial ships. The live oak trade came to a dramatic decline when wooden warships were replaced by the ironclad ships of the Civil War. The iron-clad CSS Merrimac and USS Monitor of Civil War fame were built in 1861 and 1862 respectively. However, these timberland owners retained an interest in the area by selling the land to pioneer settlers and keeping the timber rights.

Earliest Pioneers – Ormond Peninsula

In 1868, brothers John Andrew and Charles Bostrom came to Ormond to homestead government land. Land sold for about $2 per acre at the time and John Andrew and Charles Bostrom eventually built one of the finest residences in this area. The house was named Bosarve ("Home Place" in Swedish) on what is now Riverside Drive. Their two Swedish sisters (Mary and Helen) soon joined them, keeping an open house for travelers and new settlers making their way along the Halifax River. A little known fact is that Mathias Day stayed at Bosarve as he traveled south from St Augustine before train travel was available. Mathias Day purchased the former Williams Grant (3200 acres) from Samuel H. Williams's sister and soon began clearing land for a new settlement 7-miles south of Bosarve in the fall of 1870, later to become Daytona Beach.

The first house built by John Andrew and Charles Bostrom.

A Guide to Walk, Bike and Drive Our History

First Florida Retirement Community is Born

One of the early land sales, where timber rights were withheld, was made in the early 1870's. Three men employed by the Corbin Lock Company of New Britain, Connecticut traveled south from St Augustine searching for land suitable for a retirement community. With the help of John Andrew Bostrom, they located and later purchased the Henry Yonge and Hernandez grants on the west banks of the Halifax River. This brought families to Ormond searching for the perfect place to plant orange groves. Remembering home, they named the settlement New Britain in 1875.

John Anderson migrated to Florida from Maine during this period. Born in Portland, Maine in 1853, Anderson was a descendent of a wealthy family associated with rail transportation development in Maine. In the mid 1870's, John was working as a banker when he received a letter from his cousin, Samuel Dow, an early New Britain settlement resident. Samuel Dow praised the Halifax Country so much that John visited him and made arrangements to purchase 80-acres of property on the peninsula (on the east side of

Ormond Beach Historic Places

the Halifax River). This land was just north of John Andrew Bostrom's, Bosarve. Anderson's first home, "Trappers Lodge," was located in the "wilds" of the peninsula. Soon he cultivated a citrus plantation along the Halifax River and named it "Santa Lucia" after a popular Italian melody. This plantation later became a much visited destination for guests at the yet to be conceived Hotel Ormond.

Other early pioneers brought to the New Britain settlement by the Corbin Lock Company included the McNary family and the Dix sisters. These two families were highly involved in the early politics of New Britain. It was at the Dix sisters' home on April 22, 1880 that a meeting of the citizens took place to decide if the town should be incorporated and remain New Britain.

Shown below is a hand-made copy of the original Ormond family coat of arms now displayed at the Anderson-Price Memorial Library Building.

John Anderson, John Andrew Bostrom and James Ormond III became friends during this period. In fact, James Ormond III had recently visited Bosarve. This visit is said to have been instrumental in the town being renamed because John Anderson and John Andrew Bostrom convincingly swayed the colony to name it Ormond in honor of the James Ormond family. It was also agreed that the banana tree be adopted in the original city's town seal with the inscription "Ormond, Florida, Incorporated April 22nd, 1880" inserted in a circle.

A Guide to Walk, Bike and Drive Our History

Isolation Continues Until the Railroad Arrives

Travel to and from Ormond prior to the railroad was limited to parts of Old Kings Road on the mainland and the Savannah Trail on the peninsula. Buck's Stage route was established about 1882 from St. Augustine to Ormond and Daytona, via the Kings Road three times a week delivering mail, passengers and supplies. Crossing rivers along the route was accomplished by ferry or sailboat until the coming of the St. Johns and Halifax Railroad in 1886.

St. Johns and Halifax Railroad Arriving in Ormond - 1886.

In 1887 the first wooden bridge across the Halifax River (financed by Stephen Van Cullen White) was built in Ormond under the direction of John Andrew Bostrom. This narrow wooden bridge opened the mainland up to the peninsula and stimulated rapid growth, with plans of becoming the next winter vacation capital.

The Hotel Ormond is Built

Entrepreneurs like John Anderson and Joseph Price were well aware of Henry Flagler's intention of becoming a railroad tycoon with thoughts of building a standard gauge railroad and accompanying grand hotels all the way down the east coast of Florida to the Keys. With this in mind, they acquired part of the Bostrom land on his peninsula homestead and built the first 75-room wing of the Hotel Ormond.

Built in 1887, the Hotel Ormond Opens on Jan 1, 1888.

Much of the land needed for the Hotel Ormond was located along the Halifax River at a point where the John Anderson and Andrew Bostrom properties came together and was to become the focal point for development on the Halifax River in 1887. The community celebrated the opening of the Hotel Ormond on January 1, 1888 and wintering in beautiful Ormond by the affluent and health conscious had begun in earnest.

A Guide to Walk, Bike and Drive Our History

Henry Morrison Flagler Returns to St Augustine

By 1878, Flagler's wife, who had always struggled with health problems, was very ill. On advice from Mary's physician, she and Flagler visited Jacksonville, Florida for the winter. Mary's illness grew worse, however, and she died on May 18, 1881 at age 47. Two years after Mary's death, Flagler married Ida Alice Shrouds. Soon after their wedding, the couple traveled to St. Augustine, Florida where they found the city charming, but the hotel facilities and transportation systems inadequate. Flagler recognized Florida's potential to attract out-of-state visitors. Though Flagler remained on the Board of Directors of Standard Oil, he gave up his day-to-day involvement in the corporation in order to pursue his interests in Florida. Henry Morrison Flagler returned to St. Augustine in 1885 and began construction on the 540-room Hotel Ponce de Leon.

Henry Flagler's Influence is Great News

Realizing the need for a sound transportation system to support his hotel ventures, Flagler purchased the Jacksonville, St. Augustine & Halifax Railroad, the first railroad in what would eventually become the Florida East Coast Railway.

Ormond Beach Historic Places

Henry Flagler's Hotel Ponce de Leon (shown above) opened January 10, 1888 in St Augustine and was an instant success.

While in St. Augustine he built two hotels, the Ponce de Leon and the Alcazar, and purchased the third from a competitor, renaming it the Cordova.

Two years later, Flagler expanded his Florida holdings. He built a railroad bridge across the St. Johns River to gain access to the southern half of the state and purchased the Hotel Ormond for a reported sum of $112,500. This purchase allowed Flagler to quickly expand south of St Augustine and continue his railroad and hotel development activities onward towards Key West.

A Time of Growth

The later years of the 19th century proved to be a time of growth. Florida, like the rest of the country, was experiencing the industrial revolution and all that came with it, thanks to industrialists like Henry Flagler. The Jacksonville, St. Augustine & Halifax Railroad served the northeastern portion of the state and become the Florida East Coast Railway Company. When purchased by Flagler, the railroad stretched only between South Jacksonville and St. Augustine and lacked a depot sufficient to accommodate travelers to his newly built St. Augustine resorts. Flagler then built a modern depot facility as well as schools, hospitals and churches, systematically revitalizing the largely abandoned historic city.

Flagler next purchased three additional existing railroads, the St. John's Railway, the St. Augustine and Palatka Railway, and the St. Johns and Halifax Railroad so that he could provide extended rail service on standard gauge tracks to the south of St Augustine. Through determined management of these three newly purchased railroads, by spring 1889 Flagler's standard railroad system offered service from Jacksonville to Ormond and Daytona. A connecting railroad bridge was constructed in 1890 just south of the early Granada foot traffic bridge to accommodate Hotel Ormond guests on the Ormond peninsula, some of which traveled to Ormond in their own train cars.

A Guide to Walk, Bike and Drive Our History

Under Flagler's ownership, the Hotel Ormond was expanded through the years to accommodate up to 600 guests and became one of his most fashionable winter resorts, especially with winter guests seeking the warmer winter climates and exciting activities promoted by the Hotel Ormond management team. The Hotel Ormond managers coordinated activities and events and a variety of entertainment for their guests both on and off the premises. Anderson and Price, the former hotel proprietors, began a new business of providing tours of the area on the Tomoka River. Cruises departing from the hotel served picnic lunches at a river cabin on the Tomoka River. These picnic lunches and ice cream were delivered to the cabin overland from the hotel.

Many activities were provided for Hotel Ormond guests including, river excursions, horseback riding, beach racing, carriage rides and even Afro carriage rides throughout the Santa Lucia orchards via the arbor. Ormond was a beautiful and exciting destination and the word spread throughout the country and even the world.

Ormond Beach, "The Birthplace of Speed" is Born

Anderson and Price were also instrumental in the development of Ormond's "Birthplace of Speed" reputation. In 1902 they hired W.J. Morgan to promote racing on the beach. The first speed trial was run on the beach in that year. The beach proved to be the ideal racecourse and over the years a number of famous drivers tested their courage in this newfound sport of auto racing on Ormond's hard packed sand beaches.

During these early racing days, the green-shingled Ormond Garage was financed by Henry Flagler and built to accommodate early race cars. In this garage the race cars were assembled, modified, serviced and even prayed over. Some of the drivers slept with their cars or in tents outside the garage. It is said that Henry Ford had to sleep on the beach during his first visit to Ormond because he couldn't afford a room in the hotel.

John D. Rockefeller Comes to Town

Of course, a look at Ormond's history would not be complete without mentioning one of the most famous residents: John D. Rockefeller. Mr. Rockefeller, of Standard Oil fame, stated that he would live to be 100 years old. Determined to accomplish this, he became a "health advocate " before it was fashionable. He sent his employees to find the most pollution-free place to spend his winters in retirement. They chose Ormond.

In 1914 John D. Rockefeller arrived at the Hotel Ormond and rented an entire floor for him and his staff. After four winter seasons at the hotel, he purchased the home built by Reverend Harwood Huntington, whose wife was the daughter of the creator of the Pullman Train Car Company. Rockefeller's new home became known as "The Casements," and now served as his winter cottage. The Casements was located only a few hundred yards south of the Hotel Ormond, across Granada Blvd.

Through the years, Ormond residents became accustomed to having the "world's richest man" as a neighbor. Rockefeller liked being referred to as "Neighbor John" and handed out shiny new dimes as a token of his appreciation. Visitors to see Mr. Rockefeller in Ormond included such popular personalities-of-the- day as the Prince of Wales, Henry Ford and Will Rogers – to name just a few!

Each winter he held the annual Rockefeller Christmas Party at The Casements. He invited his Ormond friends to sit around the tree, share gifts and holiday cheer. Singing Christmas Carols with his friends was a favorite pastime for John D. Rockefeller. Although it was believed that

Rockefeller would live to see 100 years, he died in 1937 at the age of 97 while sleeping in The Casements, his home for over 19 years. After his death, his family put the house up for sale. Rockefeller himself might have been lost to Ormond, but the pride and prestige of his time here was not lost.

Wintering in Florida Declines

In the meantime, Ormond Beach's reputation as a fashionable winter resort center began to decline. By the outbreak of World War II, the wealthy were vacationing in Palm Beach or on Jekyll Island.

Both the Hotel Ormond and The Casements saw drastic changes in the next forty years. By 1970, the hotel's ownership changed three times. With new management came new roles. The Casements, sold by the Rockefellers in 1939, also passed from owner to owner numerous times within the next forty years becoming a girls' preparatory school and a home for the elderly. In 1959 the Ormond Hotel Corporation purchased the property with plans for development. Unfortunately, they never materialized. In 1973 The Casements was purchased by the City of Ormond Beach. Today, after its restoration, it serves the City as a cultural and community center managed by the Leisure Services Department.

Not all of the structures discussed previously have survived. Bosarve, in later years known as the San Souci Hotel, on Riverside Drive is gone as is the grand Hotel Ormond. The famous Ormond Garage burned to the ground in 1976. Some have remained, however, such as the home of the Dix sisters, and the Anderson-Price Memorial Library Building. We have included current information on over 35 historical sites and structures with a glimpse into our past, in the pages of this book.

Ormond Beach celebrated its centennial in 1980 with a pageant and many special events. In little over 100 years since the original settlement of New Britain, the City has grown from about 900 acres to more than 15,000 – and is still growing. Ormond Beach struggles with new development and many of our historical homes and sites are threatened with demolition.

A Guide to Walk, Bike and Drive Our History

The GOOD NEWS Is Presented In The Pages Of This Book.

The good news is that there are many individuals, historic preservation organizations, civic associations and government officials concerned with integrating our wonderful heritage into community projects ensuring preservation of our colorful past as we shape our dynamic future.

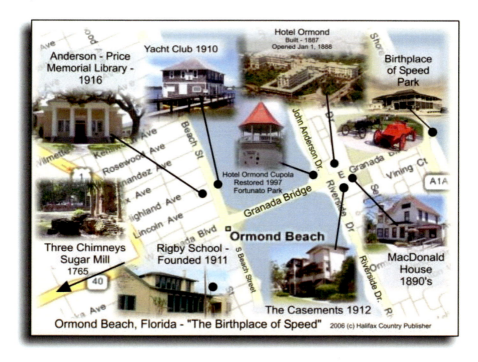

Ormond Beach Historic Places Postcard.

Alice and I hope you enjoy your travels through the streets and sites of Ormond Beach, Florida. We have but just begun the journey through our most wonderful history and welcome all passengers to join us.

Ormond Beach Historic Places

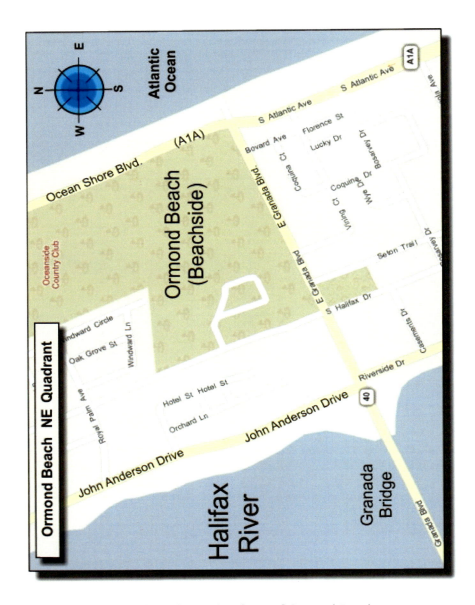

Map of Northeast Quadrant of Ormond Beach.

A Guide to Walk, Bike and Drive Our History

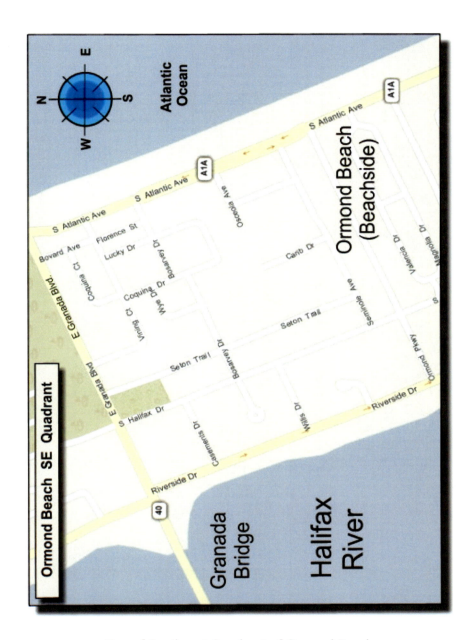

Map of Southeast Quadrant of Ormond Beach.

Ormond Beach Historic Places

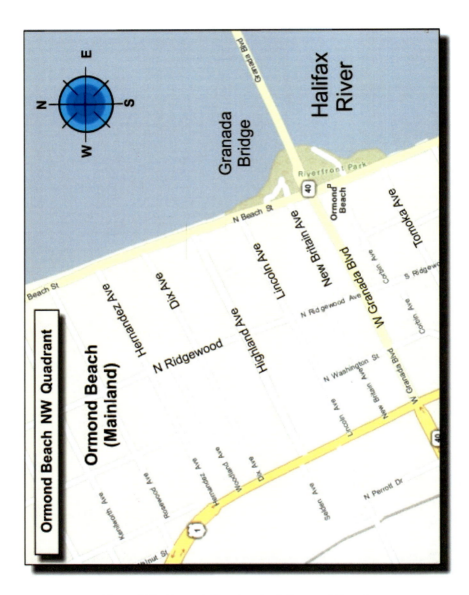

Map of Northwest Quadrant of Ormond Beach.

A Guide to Walk, Bike and Drive Our History

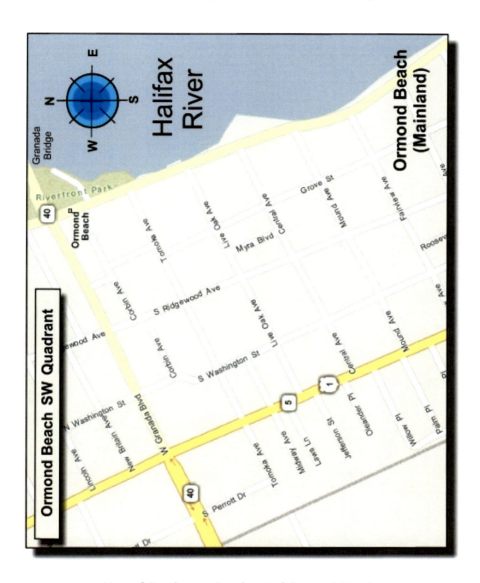

Map of Southwest Quadrant of Ormond Beach.

Ormond Beach Historic Places

The Casements

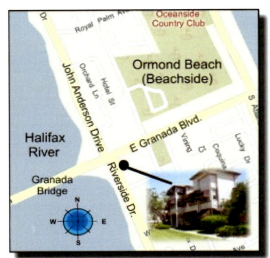

25 Riverside Dr., Ormond Beach.

The Casements is on the National Register of Historic Places and is owned and operated by the City of Ormond Beach. It serves as a cultural and civic center. The Casements Guild members provide guided tours, and a unique gift shop is on the premises.

A City Owned Public Building

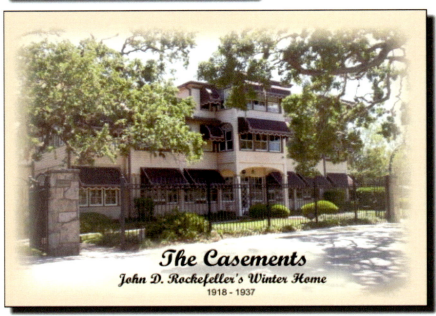

The Casements 2006 Postcard.

A Guide to Walk, Bike and Drive Our History

The Casements

Dr. and Mrs. Harwood Huntington built their winter home, The Casements, on Riverside Drive in 1912. In 1918 it would become the home of John D. Rockefeller, reputed to be the richest man in the world. Rockefeller, on the advice of his doctors, moved to Ormond Beach because of its healthy climate. He purchased The Casements in 1918 and spent his winters there until his death in 1937.

Rockefeller enlarged the house, enclosed the porches and installed an elevator. There were eight guest bedrooms and baths on the second floor, and four bedrooms and baths on the third floor. Also on the property was a large garage with two apartments above, and a shop building containing a water softening plant, central oil burning heating and a hot water system. The superintendent, Fred Perrin and his wife lived in a nine-room cottage. Additionally, a greenhouse and a potting room were a part of the property.

Rockefeller enjoyed living at The Casements, and preferred it to his more spacious and ornate homes in New York and New Jersey. It suited his lifestyle to live quietly and healthily in Ormond Beach and play golf on the Hotel Ormond golf course. He liked to be known as "Neighbor John". He would come down by train in early winter, and if it was a chilly day, he would be wearing a long overcoat, scarf and cloth cap with earmuffs. A small group of local citizens would greet him at the station and he would hand out dimes to everyone, a custom he maintained throughout his life.

The most outstanding social occasion at The Casements was Rockefeller's annual Christmas party, when a few personal friends and long time neighbors were invited to join him in the holiday celebration. The Casements was brilliantly decorated with lighted candles in the windows. A huge Christmas tree was in the center of the living room with a huge pile of gifts under it. A men's quartet from the Daytona Beach Lion's Club sang Christmas carols. Rockefeller would help distribute gifts to his guests, but when the time came for ice cream and cake, he would retire to his room.

Ormond Beach Historic Places

Fortunato Park and the Hotel Ormond Cupola

Corner of John Anderson Drive and Granada Avenue, at the base of the Granada Bridge.

Fortunato Park was named in honor of Mayor Nicholas Fortunato who served for 10 years. It was dedicated in his memory in 1997.

The red roofed cupola that is now on display in Fortunato Park has become the park's centerpiece. It originally graced the Hotel Ormond for over 100 years.

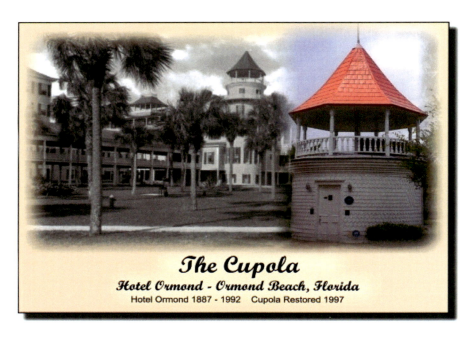

The Cupola 2006 Postcard.

A Guide to Walk, Bike and Drive Our History

Fortunato Park and The Hotel Ormond Cupola

The red roofed cupola that is now on display in Fortunato Park (named after Mayor Nicholas Fortunato who served for 10 years) has become the park's centerpiece. It originally graced the Hotel Ormond for over 100 years. John Anderson and Joseph Price built the grand hotel in 1887 and the opening day was January 1, 1888. The Hotel Ormond was a wooden structure originally with only 75 rooms. Eventually purchased by Henry Flagler for $112,500 in 1890 it was enlarged to over 300 rooms.

The Hotel, was located on 80 acres and included cottages, garage, hot house, golf course, swimming pool, power plant, laundry facility and servants quarters. The grounds encompassed land from the Halifax River to the west and the Atlantic Ocean to the east. It was located at the corner of John Anderson Drive and Granada, across from Fortunato Park and where the Ormond Heritage Condominium now stands.

The Hotel Ormond became one of the most famous in the world, to which the rich and famous came to be seen. Many guests including John D. Rockefeller, Harriet Beecher Stowe, the Prince of Wales (Duke of Windsor) Henry Ford, Thomas Edison, and even gangster Al Capone enjoyed its luxurious food, accommodations, service, and entertainment.

Unfortunately, in 1992 the Hotel Ormond was demolished, but the combined efforts of the Ormond Beach Historical Trust, Inc., and the City of Ormond Beach were able to save the cupola from the wrecking ball. Five years later the refurbished cupola found a home in the newly developed Fortunato Park.

Today, the Ormond Beach Historical Trust oversees the cupola and a mural, pictures and memorabilia are on display inside the building.

Ormond Beach Historic Places

Talahloka

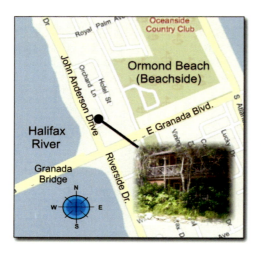

Located at 19 Orchard Lane. From East Granada Blvd. turn north on John Anderson Drive (at Fortunato Park) and within 1 block, turn right on Orchard Lane. About halfway down the lane look on the left and you will see Talahloka at 19 Orchard lane.

National Register of Historic Places

A Private Home

Talahloka – 19 Orchard Lane, Ormond Beach

A Guide to Walk, Bike and Drive Our History

Talahloka

John Anderson built the original cabin for use as a hunting Lodge. Talahloka, was built of palmetto logs in a wooded environment on John Anderson's Santa Lucia plantation.

Erected just north of the Hotel Ormond, many guests took up residence there when the hotel was full. Some took their meals at the hotel, while others employed a cook.

Talahloka Hunting Lodge shown in the early 1900's.

Talahloka, built in the 1880's, is a frame vernacular building, 2 stories tall with a veranda surrounding it on three sides, in the style of the Adirondack Mountain structures. Each of the two floors has four rooms surrounding a central fireplace that has eight openings.

Ormond Beach Historic Places

Trappers Lodge

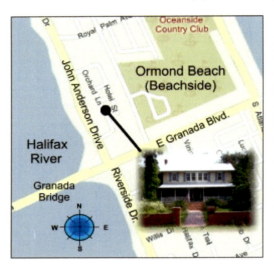

Located at 65 Orchard Lane. From East Granada Blvd. turn north on John Anderson Drive (at Fortunato Park) and within 1 block, turn right on Orchard Lane. Follow Orchard lane to the left and you will see Trappers Lodge at 65 Orchard lane on the right hand side a few homes after the turn.

A Private Home

Trappers Lodge - 65 Orchard Lane.

A Guide to Walk, Bike and Drive Our History

Trappers Lodge

John Anderson migrated to Florida from Maine during the late 1870's period. He, too, settled on the east side of the Halifax River. His first home, "Trappers Lodge," was located in the "wilds" of the peninsula. John Anderson built Trappers Lodge in 1876 and it acquired its name because a deer carcass usually hung outside. Later he expanded his plantation on the Halifax River and named it "Santa Lucia" after a popular Italian melody.

Trappers Lodge began as a one room log cabin and a fireplace. Another cabin was added later with a breezeway that connected the two with a fireplace at each end.

Since 1911, when John Anderson died, a second floor and other rooms were added and the exterior changed and brought up to date.

Early Trappers Lodge - 65 Orchard Lane.

71 Orchard Lane

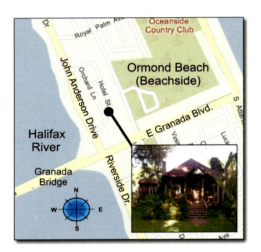

Located at 71 Orchard Lane. From East Granada Blvd. turn north on John Anderson Drive (at Fortunato Park) and within 1 block, turn right on Orchard Lane. Follow Orchard Lane to the left and you will see 71 Orchard Lane on the right hand side a few homes after the turn.

A Private Home

71 Orchard Lane, Ormond Beach

A Guide to Walk, Bike and Drive Our History

71 Orchard Lane

John Anderson constructed this frame vernacular "hunting lodge" in the mid 1880's.

The palm logs used in construction of the exterior walls, which are chinked or filled with plaster in places, are placed in a vertical instead of the traditional horizontal style. The cement like material that holds the cabbage palm logs of the building together has crumbled in places revealing a tightly wadded insulation of Spanish Moss. It is said that the squirrels pull the moss out to build their nests.

Commander Edward Fischer and his wife Sarah restored this house.

Located at 71 Orchard Lane.

Ormond Beach Historic Places

Nathan Cobb Cottage

Located at 137 Orchard Lane

From East Granada Blvd. turn north on John Anderson Drive (at Fortunato Park) and within 1 block, turn right on Orchard Lane. Follow Orchard Lane to the left and you will see 137 Orchard Lane on the right hand side, a few homes after the turn.

A Private Home

Nathan Cobb Cottage, November 2006.

A Guide to Walk, Bike and Drive Our History

Nathan Cobb Cottage

On December 5, 1896, the 500-ton schooner "Nathan F. Cobb" grounded itself on a sandbar off the coast of Ormond Beach, on its way from Georgia to New York. She encountered a "nor'easter", began to leak and became unstable. The Nathan Cobb had already lost the main and mizzenmast plus two crew off the North Carolina coast. After 3-1/2 days of drifting, she became grounded at Ormond.

William Fagen received permission to salvage the timber and built this modest three-room cottage at Santa Lucia plantation. The exterior was built of the cargo of railroad ties and the masts were cut and split into shingles. The ship's railings were used for porch decorations and the two ship's knees became the framework for the front door.

Later owners have included Mary Chase, Amelia Fowler, George Wendell and Mr. and Mrs. Archibald Trimble. Many changes to the cottage have been made over the years.

Nathan Cobb Cottage - 137 Orchard Lane, Ormond Beach.

Ormond Beach Historic Places

Ormond Garage

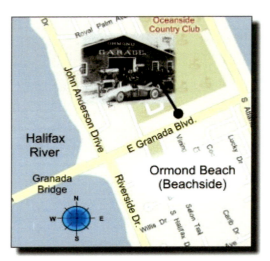

Originally located at 113 East Granada Blvd. now the Sun-Trust Bank site. As you come over the Granada Bridge from the mainland heading east, 113 E Granada is on the left just past Halifax Drive.

Commemorative Plaque

A commemorative plaque (in front of the Sun Trust Bank) designates the location of the famous Ormond Garage.

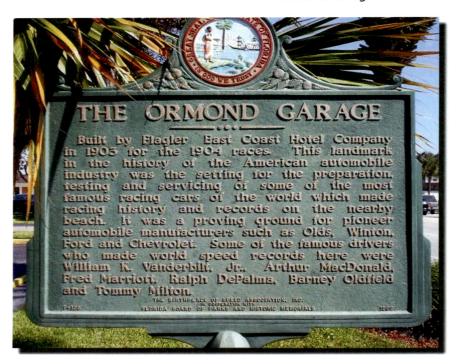

A Guide to Walk, Bike and Drive Our History

Ormond Garage

Henry Flagler built the Ormond Garage on Hotel Ormond property in 1903, for the 1904 races on the hard packed sands of the beach. The building was a long, one story, shingled, peaked roof structure with a brick floor. The green- sided garage housed 100 automobiles brought to Ormond by men like Olds, Winton, Ford, and Chevrolet who manufactured the cars. Inside the garage, the cars were prepared for the races as mechanics worked on the engines.

This building called "Gasoline Alley" unfortunately burned to the ground, in one hour, in 1976. However, it played an important role in the life of Ormond's races on the beach, and in Ormond's designation as "The Birthplace of Speed". Drivers who set world speed records included Vanderbilt, Marriott, DePalma, Oldfield and Milton.

A cypress-shingled building was erected behind the Ormond Garage to house chauffeurs of wealthy guests who came in later years. Also on the property was a laundry building where thousands of linens of all description were washed and dried. Behind the laundry were dormitories for men and women employees.

Original Ormond Garage Built in 1903.

The Birthplace of Speed Park

Located on the beach where Granada Blvd. meets A1A, the Birthplace of Speed Park displays the two replicas of the first sanctioned automobile race on the beach. The two replicas glisten in the Florida sunshine inviting everyone to share in our early history. Ormond Beach is truly The Birthplace of Speed. Winton's red Bullet barely won the race by 2-tenths of a second.

A Public Park

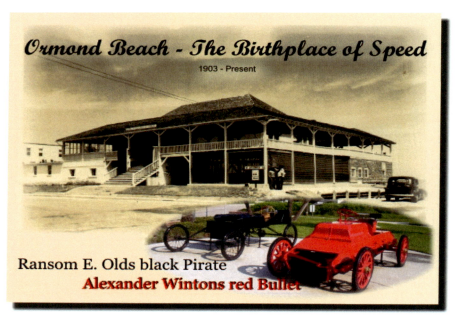

Birthplace of Speed Park Postcard, 2006

A Guide to Walk, Bike and Drive Our History

The Birthplace of Speed Park

Racing on Ormond Beach started in 1902 with the discovery that the hard packed sand would support early automobiles. The city's famous connection with racing actually began in 1903 when the Winton Bullet won a Challenge Cup against the Olds Pirate by two-tenths of a second.

American records were set that year, and the world took notice, as chronicled below.

In 1904 speed tournaments including one for motorcycles set world's records that lasted for seven years.

In 1905, the Stanley Rocket, designed and built by F. E. Stanley recorded many wins and near-wins and became known as the most aerodynamic racer of the day.

Fred Marriott drove F. E. Stanley's Rocket Racer in 1906 and set the mark that became Ormond Beach's most famous land speed record. The incredible speed of 127.659 mph endured for four years.

In 1910 the Marriott record was broken by 4mph as Barney Oldfield raced the Lightning Benz at 131.75 mph.

For eight years Ormond Beach was the world's center of racing. Inventors with familiar names like Olds, Winton, Ford, Chevrolet, Stanley and Packard tested their machines on the only reliable, flat track in the United States. Ormond became known as "The Birthplace of Speed".

During the Speed Centennial in 2003, several thousand watched 50 of the worlds greatest antique, race cars race again, and the new Birthplace of Speed Park was rededicated with historic markers and replicas of the 1903 Winton Bullet and Old's Pirate.

Ormond is proud of its heritage as "The Birthplace of Speed" and continues to celebrate with an annual Antique Car Show and nighttime Gaslight Parade on Thanksgiving Day weekend.

Nathan Cobb Shipwreck

Located at 621 S A1A (Inside Casa Del Mar Beach Resort pool area)

From East Granada Blvd. turn south on A1A and travel about 2-miles south to 621 S A1A, at Cardinal Ave. The Nathan Cobb historical plaque is inside the Casa Del Mar pool area.

Nathan Cobb Shipwreck Plaque - 621 South A1A.

A Guide to Walk, Bike and Drive Our History

Nathan Cobb Shipwreck

On December 5, 1896, the 500-ton schooner Nathan F. Cobb grounded itself on the sands of Ormond Beach. The schooner had lost its masts and the last six men of her crew awaited rescue from the cold.

The Nathan Cobb schooner carried a crew of eight and a load of railroad cross ties when she left port. She encountered a "nor'easter", began to leak and became unstable. The Nathan Cobb had already lost the main and mizzenmast plus two crew off the North Carolina coast. After 3-1/2 days of drifting, she became grounded at Ormond.

Two boats were launched toward the survivors as a crowd on the beach watched intently. Five times the boats carrying two men and ropes attempted a rescue, but were unsuccessful. Unfortunately, one man attempting the rescue, Freed Waterhouse, lost his life.

Ormond Beach Historic Places

Nathan Cobb Shipwreck

Finally the captain of the Nathan Cobb went overboard with a line from the schooner. A boat from shore was able to pick him up. The rope the captain used to come ashore was tied to one on shore with a life preserver attached to it. The preserver was sent out on the line to each crewmember and they were brought to shore safely.

In 1897, a monument to Waterhouse was erected in the dunes near the wreck site to commemorate his bravery. However, in July of 1972 vandals chiseled the bronze plaque from the stone that held it. The plaque was located in the palmetto scrub in the dunes in November 1972 and it is now safe and secure on the east side of the Casa Del Mar Motel near the shipwreck site.

A Guide to Walk, Bike and Drive Our History

Nathan Cobb Shipwreck

It should also be noted that a large wooden telephone pole has been located at the Nathan Cobb shipwreck site to identify the location and warn swimmers about possible ship wreckage debris still visible on the ocean floor at low tide.

Timber from the wreck was salvaged and a three-room cottage was built on Orchard Lane called the Nathan Cobb Cottage. Please refer to the Nathan Cobb Cottage information presented earlier in this book.

Memorial Art Museum and Gardens

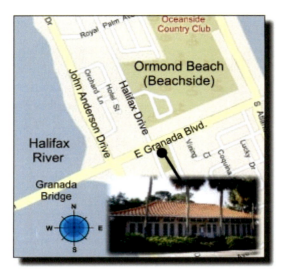

78 East Granada Blvd. Located on the SE corner of Halifax Drive and East Granada Blvd. Also visit Emmons Cottage located at the rear parking area.

Open to Public

A Guide to Walk, Bike and Drive Our History

Memorial Art Museum and Gardens

The Memorial Art Museum and Gardens was founded in 1946, to honor service personnel from this area who died in WWII. A small group of citizens collected funds to house paintings and City and County officials cooperated to obtain property for the purpose.

There was a small building on the property and this was used as an entrance to a fireproof gallery, which was constructed in the rear of the building to house the paintings. The art gallery was named the Ormond War Memorial Art Gallery and a bronze memorial plaque listing 147 names of local men and women of the armed services is in the lobby of the museum. Another plaque listing three men of Ormond who lost their lives in World War I is the southeast corner of the Memorial Garden.

The Museum houses the paintings of Malcolm Fraser. A collection of symbolic religious paintings, this body of work is the largest collection of its kind by one artist in the world. The Museum also displays the works of established and budding Florida artists.

In an oasis behind the Museum, a 4-acre botanical garden is nestled where exotic plants (from Africa, South America and the Caribbean) and indigenous plants flourish. Strolling the nature paths, past lily ponds, peacock fountain, bridges, and gazebo is a special treat in this lovely oasis on East Granada Blvd.

Emmons Cottage

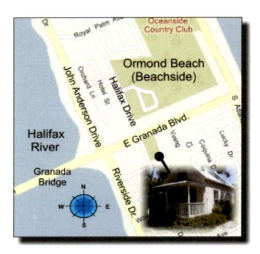

78 E. Granada Boulevard Now located on the grounds of the Memorial Art Museum at the rear parking lot, just off Seton Trail. From the Granada Bridge going east on Granada Blvd. turn right just past the Ormond Beach Art Museum on Seton Trail. Just past the botanical gardens on the right, turn right into the rear parking lot and you will see Emmons Cottage on the right.

Emmons Cottage located just behind the Memorial Art Museum.

A Guide to Walk, Bike and Drive Our History

Emmons Cottage

The Emmons Cottage was built in 1885 of native Florida pine (Fat Lighter Pine) that is termite resistant.

Folk Victorian Architecture is the style of the Emmons Cottage. The cottage is a total of 994 square feet, 2 rooms on the first floor and 2 smaller rooms upstairs.

For 40 years the house sat empty at 150 N. Beach, at the SW corner of Dix Street and N Beach Street. The 10,000- pound Emmons Cottage was saved from demolition in May 1998 and moved to its present location in the gardens at the Memorial Art Museum and Gardens. The move cost $8,000 and $10,000 more was raised to accomplish refurbishments.

The porch and windows have been restored and a new aluminum roof installed. Period furniture has been added to enhance an important piece of Florida history. Please check at the Art Museum for visiting hours.

Turning left into the Art Museum rear parking lot off Seton Trail.

Ormond Beach Historic Places

Billy's Tap Room & Grill

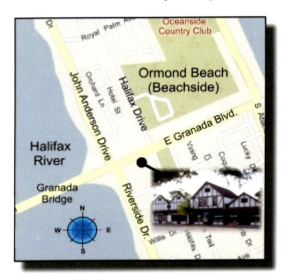

58 East Granada Blvd. Located right across from the Ormond Beach Post Office. When traveling east on Granada Blvd after crossing the Granada Bridge, Billy's is located on the right just before Halifax Drive.

Open to the Public

Billy's Tap Room & Grill - 58 East Granada Blvd.

Billy's Tap Room & Grill

The English Pub features a maple bar and high backed booths. Ormond Beach's oldest, award winning restaurant displays photos of historic Ormond and the many celebrities it has entertained.

Billy's Tap Room and Grill actually began as a gift shop and tea room on the property of the beautiful Hotel Ormond in 1922. The owners of the hotel knew Billy MacDonald, in New York City, where he was the manager of all lounges within the Astor and Plaza Hotels. They asked Billy to come to Ormond Beach. The hotel opened each year the Sunday after Halloween, and remained open through Easter Sunday. Liking the area so well, Billy purchased the building, currently known as Billy's Tap Room & Grill, at 58 E. Granada Boulevard, in 1926. As best that can be determined, the building was constructed in 1910 and operated as a Drug Store. The MacDonald family moved upstairs and occupied the upper floor until 1939

Later they purchased the property, currently known as the "MacDonald House," for $3,900. The MacDonald house remained their home for many years.

MacDonald House

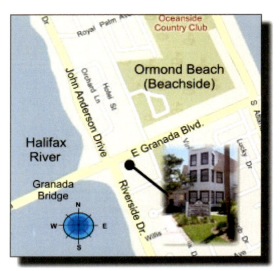

Located at 38 East Granada Blvd. just across from the Ormond Beach Post Office. The MacDonald House serves as the Ormond Beach Welcome Center and office for the City run Tennis Center.

Open to the Public

MacDonald House - 38 East Granada Blvd.

A Guide to Walk, Bike and Drive Our History

MacDonald House

Originally built about 1900, the MacDonald House is a beautiful 2-1/2 story Queen Anne style house. The house was appraised in 1933 at $2500, plus $1000 for the land, for a total of $3500.00.

The MacDonald house contained a shop, dining room kitchen, bedroom and bedroom closet on the first floor, three bedrooms, sitting room and closet on the second floor, plus two attic bedrooms. Probably the attic bedrooms were for servants. All rooms appear to have been well furnished.

In May 1939, William and Elizabeth MacDonald purchased the house and the building became known as "The MacDonald House". William MacDonald established the popular Billy's Tap Room & Grill in 1926, just a few doors east of the MacDonald House.

Between 1964 and 1970 the property was involved in several transactions. During the 1970's the property was acquired by the City of Ormond Beach. In 1999 the land was valued at $789,250 and the building at $107,869 for a total of $897,019.

In the 1990's, the Ormond Beach Historical Trust and preservationists saved the house from destruction. Funds from the State of Florida, from the City of Ormond Beach and donations in the amount of $140,700 were spent in the effort.

The city of Ormond Beach Tennis Center operates from the MacDonald House. The Tennis Center staff occupies a small office in the rear that was once the kitchen and dinning room.

The Ormond Beach Historical Trust currently operates a Welcome Center and gift shop from the ground floor offices.

Ormond Beach Historic Places

Riverway

Located at 127 Riverside Drive.

Traveling across the E. Granada Bridge on Granada Blvd. turn right at the base of the bridge on Riverside Drive. You will pass The Casements on your left and begin the beautiful narrow drive south along what was once Bosarve.

National Register of Historic Places

Private Home

Riverway Located at 127 Riverside Drive.

A Guide to Walk, Bike and Drive Our History

Riverway

Riverway, so named for its proximity to the Halifax River, is an elegant Mediterranean style home with light, airy, spacious rooms, pinewood floors and high ceiling. Seven fireplaces, a dumbwaiter and a 1912 grand piano grace its rooms. Cypress and heart of pine were used to construct the home and a basement at ground level makes it unusual. The basement walls are made of boards from packing cases that bear the names of John D. Rockefeller and his housekeeper in script on them. Mr. Rockefeller purchased the house to accommodate staff and guests.

John D. Rockefeller sold the house to Albert Frederick Wilson a co-founder of the School of Journalism at Columbia. Sloan Wilson, son of Albert Frederick Wilson, authored the best sellers, "The Man In The Grey Flannel Suit", and "Summer Place".

Mrs. Wilson was from a wealthy Maine family and she authored 3 books. One of the visitors she entertained at Riverway was Mary M. Bethune, founder of Bethune-Cookman College in Daytona Beach.

Mr. Albert Wilson founded a school in Daytona Beach and also attended to the orange grove on his property.

Four of the Wilson's 8 servants lived in quarters in the basement at Riverway. The other servants left to cross the bridge from the peninsula to the mainland at dusk because black people were not allowed on the peninsula after dark.

Ormond Beach Historic Places

Bosarve

Located at 195 Riverside Drive.

Traveling across the E. Granada Bridge on Granada Blvd. turn right at the base of the bridge on Riverside Drive. You will pass The Casements on your left and begin the beautiful drive south along the narrow Riverside Drive, for about 2-blocks.

Historic Marker only

(Bosarve was demolished 1967)

Bosarve (Historic Marker) - 195 Riverside Drive.

A Guide to Walk, Bike and Drive Our History

Bosarve

The first white settlers of Ormond Beach were John Andrew Bostrom and his brother Charles. They were born on Gottland, a Swedish island in the Baltic Sea. John Andrew Bostrom and Charles Bostrom received deeded land in 1868 at $2.00 per acre, and the first dwelling that they built was a palmetto shack.

The second house was a two story frame house. The main part (kitchen) was built in 1869. Shingles were homemade and bricks for the chimney were taken from old plantation ruins. Boards from dry goods boxes were nailed on the inside studding and then pasted over with newspapers. Access to building materials was limited during these early times.

Taking in borders was necessary for the Bostrom brothers John Andrew and Charles, and the Bostrom House soon became known to be the finest in Ormond. The brothers built a wharf and leveled a road to the beach that was, at the time, the only wagon road across the peninsula. They planted orange groves as well.

The third house (all on the same site) was one of the best residences in the area. It was a three story frame house and well known for boarding famous people during the winter months.

John Andrew Bostrom was a much respected citizen of Ormond having the finest orange grove in the area. He became president of the Ormond Beach Hotel Co, and owner of the Coquina Hotel. His many friends included Henry Morrison Flagler, James Ormond III, John Anderson and Joseph Price.

After John Andrew's death in 1927 at age 91, his son divided and remodeled the house, and in the 30's Bosarve became an exclusive hotel run by Mrs. Henry Oltman who renamed it Sans Souci. Jackie Kennedy Onassis and her sister wintered there with a governess. The Women's' Army Corps, during WWII, billeted there. The property was subdivided in 1946 and Bosarve was torn down. A plaque commemorates Bosarve at 195 Riverside Drive.

Ormond Beach Historic Places

Lion House

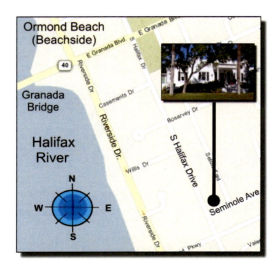

Located at 75 Seminole Ave. (corner of South Halifax Drive and Seminole Ave.) From E Granada Blvd., turn south on S Halifax Drive and the Lion House is about 3 blocks on the left.

A Private Home

Lion House – 75 Seminole Ave.

A Guide to Walk, Bike and Drive Our History

Lion House

In 1928 Mr. Henry H. Britt from Saginaw, Michigan, who was a retired curator from the Smithsonian Institute, built the Lion House.

The Lion House is unique because it was the first house in Ormond Beach to have a garage under the house. Two statuary lions grace each side of the front entrance.

Mr. John Yordi, Mr. Rockefeller's male nurse and personal bodyguard later owned the home. Mr. Yordi was Swiss and became a trusted and valuable employee to John D. Rockefeller for 20-years. He succeeded where doctors failed to preserve and protect Mr. Rockefeller's health. Mr. Yordi accompanied John D. in a special car on his last train trip north to "Golf House" a Rockefeller Residence at Lakewood, New Jersey to celebrate his 97th birthday July 8, 1936.

John D. Rockefeller died at The Casements in Ormond, May 23, 1937.

McSwain House
LaTourette
(Little Tower)

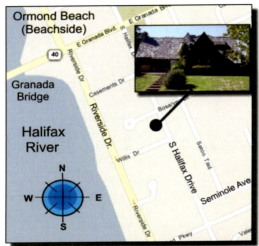

Located at 128 South Halifax Drive. From E Granada Blvd., turn south on S Halifax Drive and the McSwain House is about 2 blocks on the right.

A City of Ormond Beach Historic Site

A Private Home

McSwain House LaTourette - 128 South Halifax Drive.

A Guide to Walk, Bike and Drive Our History

McSwain House
LaTourette
(Little Tower)

Sometimes called "The Fairytale House" or "The Hansel and Gretel House", it is unusual and fascinating. Built in 1937, the City of Ormond Beach designated the house a Historic Site (a house of significance over 50 years old).

Built by Professor and Mrs. A. F. Wilson for the mother of Professor Wilson, LaTourette was once a guest house used by John D. Rockefeller. Its history included Parish House for St. James Episcopal Church and a home for a WWII army officer and his wife.

The house is of French Normandy architecture with brick construction and story- book tower. The living room has a high carved beamed cathedral ceiling and blue plaster walls with brick fireplace between 2 windows. The floors are heart of pine.

In 1952 Dr. George and Mary Jane McSwain and two sons moved into LaTourette. Mary Jane McSwain wrote a garden column for the Daytona Beach News Journal.

The McSwains added to, and remodeled the house. They landscaped the grounds, removing a circular driveway and 2 car garage. A playhouse was added in the backyard with French architecture. The palmetto-covered lot became a park like garden with tall trees, flowers, rocks, roses and citrus. A greenhouse became home to delicate plants and a patio was added for parties and picnics.

Ormond Beach Historic Places

Rowallan/Lisnaroe

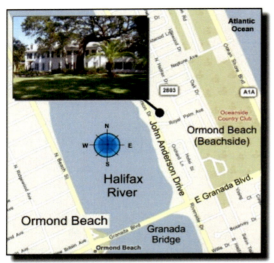

Located at 253 John Anderson Drive. From East Granada Blvd, turn north on John Anderson Drive and travel about a mile. Rowallan is located on the right, one house past Royal Palm Ave.

National Register of Historic Places

A Private Home

Rowallan/Lisnaroe - 253 John Anderson Drive.

A Guide to Walk, Bike and Drive Our History

Rowallan/Lisnaroe

The three story, white painted house was built in 1913 with six slender columns to decorate the facade. It was the winter home of Alexander Millar Lindsay. Originally a merchant from Scotland, he was a dealer in cloth and dry goods who came to the United States, partnered with two other gentlemen to begin their own successful business in Rochester, N.Y.

Attracted to the warm Florida climate, Lindsay and his family journeyed to Florida aboard their private railroad car named "Rowallan". Lindsay purchased the property at 253 John Anderson Drive and built a large, beautiful home made of heart of cypress with 28 rooms, 7 fireplaces and 7 bathrooms. The property included a caretaker's two-story cottage, a four-car garage, tool shop, attic, cellar, tennis court and laundry building.

The Lindsay family named the home after the castle of the same name near their former home in Scotland. The Lindsay family lived at Rowallan and traveled to Florida with a cook, maids, butler and chauffeur.

The house passed from the Lindsay family to the Martin family and then to Mr. & Mrs. Butts in 1936. The name, Rowallan, was changed to Lisnaroe "By The Water" in Celtic, and was the name of a property owned by Mrs. Butts grandfather in Northern Ireland. Under Mrs. Butts auspicious, Lisnaroe became a hospitable home popular for its wonderful parties.

Mrs. Butts was involved in the Volusia County Historical Commission, Garden Club of Halifax Country, Halifax Historical Society, and Daytona Beach Symphony. She helped to raise funds to preserve John D. Rockefeller's home "The Casements" in Ormond Beach.

Hammock Home

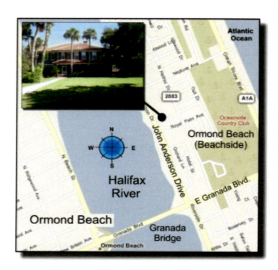

Located at 311 John Anderson Drive. From East Granada Blvd, turn north on John Anderson Drive and travel about a mile. Hammock Home is located on the right, 7 houses past Royal Palm Ave.

National Register of Historic Places

A Private Home

Hammock Home - 311 John Anderson Drive.

A Guide to Walk, Bike and Drive Our History

Hammock Home

Joseph Downing Price came from Covington, Kentucky to Ormond Beach in the early 1870's and lived in a cabin in the woods. The cabin was named Hammock Home. Joseph Price was a civil engineer, and life was harsh as he fished, hunted and rolled logs.

John Anderson also a young man migrated from Portland, Maine to the New Britain colony and lived in a cabin in the woods called Trapper's Lodge.

Once the St. Johns and Halifax River Railroad arrived in Ormond in 1886 and the bridge was built across the Halifax, Anderson & Price decided to go into the hotel business. With the help of Stephen Van Cullen White, who was the financier, the two men built the 75-room Hotel Ormond. It became a success as businessmen from the north discovered the hunting, fishing and relaxation that this area afforded them

The Hotel Ormond was managed first by Dr. S. E. Churchill with his sister and later by Anderson and Price, even after selling the inn to Henry Morrison Flagler.

Joseph Price married Mary Belle Pinkerton from Covington, Kentucky, and they had a son Hubert who became an Ormond Mayor.

Price built a small home and packing- house after moving out of his cabin and in later years built the present Hammock Home.

The house is shaded by large oak trees, has a screened in porch, and rooms with high ceilings. It sits on a slope of land on John Anderson Drive.

Ormond Beach Historic Places

Number 9 Plantation

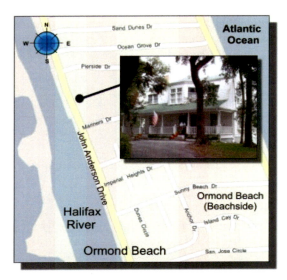

Located at 2887 John Anderson Drive.

Turn North on John Anderson Drive from Granada Blvd. and travel 5.4 miles to 2887 John Anderson Drive.

The street before Number 9 Plantation is Mariners Dr.

A Private Home

Number 9 Plantation - 2887 John Anderson Drive.

Number 9 Plantation

Chauncey Bacon's Number 9 Plantation included 172 acres of land from the Halifax River to the Atlantic Ocean. Bacon gave the name to his property after reading a story called "Seven Oaks" by J. G. Holland, published by Scribner's Magazine in 1872. The story told about a group of wanderers who gave numbers to their temporary camps and Number 9 was the last camp they made. Bacon also had considered 8 other sites before deciding on a homestead and so the name "Number 9" seemed to be the perfect name for the plantation.

Mr. Bacon, a Connecticut Yankee, wore a top hat in the woods and wilderness of the New Britain of 1876, and was known as "The Duke". The land was covered with a forest of palmettos, oaks and pine trees. Bacon cleared the land by using hand axes and hoes. Mosquitoes, gnats and sand flies bit him unmercifully. Snakes, bears, wildcats, deer and panthers roamed the dense woods.

His labor produced, at first, a palmetto thatched hut. Then, he planted a grove of tropical fruit trees. A second home was built by Mr. Bacon, that was a small cottage, and Mrs. Bacon became the first schoolteacher in New Britain.

In 1880 a ship "City of Vera Cruz" sank off shore. Mr. Bacon's third house, on the same site, used mahogany cargo from that wreck to build mantels, doors, a magnificent wooden staircase to the second story, and a massive front door. The house included a library with books on every subject including horticulture.

Soon Number 9 became famous for its wonderful jellies, jams and preserves. When the Hotel Ormond opened, the hotel guests and tourists sailed upriver to wander the groves and buy the preserves. After a rough road was built to Number 9, Hotel Ormond guests came by horseback, bicycles and carriages to make their purchases.

Bulow Plantation Ruins

Located 13 miles north of Granada Blvd. Take N Beach Street north and it becomes Old Dixie Highway. Continue on past Walter Boardman Lane for about 1.5 miles and turn right on Old Kings Road. Go about 2-miles north on Old Kings Road and look for the park entrance sign.

Historic State Park

Bulow Plantation Ruins - 13 miles north of Granada Blvd.

Bulow Plantation Ruins

The fabulous Bulow Plantation is no more. Left are the extensive coquina ruins of the great sugar mill, preserved wells, springhouse and foundations of the mansion.

The original owner, James Russell, died in 1815 and his heirs sold the property to Major Charles Wilhelm Bulow.

In 1820 Major Charles Wilhelm Bulow of Charleston, acquired nearly 6000 acres, at $9,944.50, for the production of sugar cane, cotton, indigo and rice. Three hundred slaves cleared land and erected the buildings that comprised an oasis in the wilderness. Unfortunately, three years after beginning the undertaking, Charles Bulow, age 44, was dead.

John Bulow, still a minor child, who was being educated in Paris, returned to continue the successful management of the property under a trusteeship. John lived well at Bulowville, entertaining notables such as John James Audubon.

> **BULOW SUGAR MILL**
> This was the largest sugar mill in Florida. It was operated by Charles Wilhelm Bulow and John Joachim Bulow from 1820 until it was burned by the Seminoles in 1836.
> Sugar cane was planted in January and February and was ready for harvesting by mid-October. Field workers cut the cane and loaded it on wagons that brought it to the mill for processing.

The bounty and wealth of the plantation continued until the outbreak of the Second Seminole War in 1835. In January, 1836, General Joseph Hernandez ordered Bulowville abandoned because of the great number of Indians in the area. John Bulow, with many of the settlers, expressed his disapproval of resetting the Seminoles to west of the Mississippi. Bulow was taken prisoner by the military.

The Seminoles burned Bulowville to the ground. The fires could be seen forty miles away in St. Augustine. A government document states the loss amount at $83,475. Nothing was ever paid on the claim. John Bulow never returned to rebuild. He returned to Paris where he died at the age of 26.

Fairchild Oak

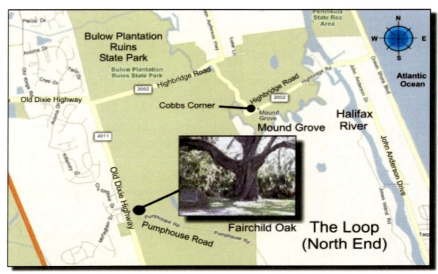

Located on the East side of Old Dixie Hwy (The Loop) Across from James Ormond Tomb. The entrance is at Pumphouse Road. **A Public Park**

The Mighty Ormond Fairchild Oak Postcard, 2006

A Guide to Walk, Bike and Drive Our History

Fairchild Oak

Live oaks were vital to America's shipbuilding industry. The tree often came in exactly the right shape for ship's frames, or knees, and was almost indestructible compared with other available woods. They were known for their strength and buoyancy and their ability to repel cannonballs. A large market existed for the trees in Europe where most of the great live oaks had long ago been cut down. "Live Oakers" filled logging carts to capacity and hauled logs to rivers for shipment to support this flourishing industry.

Nicknamed "Old Ironsides", the USS Constitution was built from the early Florida Live Oak.

The live oak on the Damietta Plantation survived being cut for the ship building trade because of its proximity to the home of James Ormond.

The Fairchild Oak measures 24 feet in circumference, 68 feet tall and 133 feet at its crown.

It is the 15th largest tree in Florida. Dr. David Fairchild, for whom the tree is named, thought the tree to be a cross between a live and laurel oak.

Tomb of James Ormond II

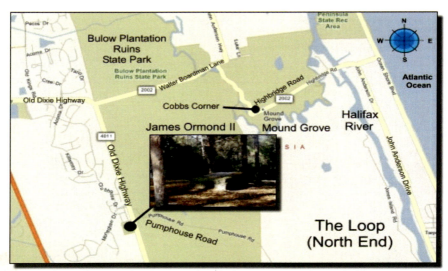

Located 9 miles north of Granada Blvd. on N. Beach St. (Old Dixie Highway)   Now called Ormond Park.   **A Public Park**

Tomb of James Ormond II.

A Guide to Walk, Bike and Drive Our History

Tomb of James Ormond II

A most interesting and important plantation family was that of James Ormond. Captain James Ormond I owned an armed brig the "Somerset" in the late 1700's that traded between Savannah and Apalachicola, the West Indies, and Europe. After his retirement from the sea, he planted cotton on the Island of Exuma. He then came to Florida to obtain a land grant. He received two 1000 acre land grants from the Spanish. A runaway slave killed him.

James Ormond II settled on his father's land grants and after fleeing a debtor's prison in the Baltic, established Damietta plantation before the Seminole War.

James Ormond II died on the plantation and was buried there in 1829. His 13 year old son, James Ormond III, erected the tomb of James Ormond II

The inscription on the Tombstone reads:

**James Ormond
Died Sept 30th
1829
An Honest Man**

James Ormond III fought in the Second Seminole Indian War by joining the "Mosquito Roarers". He received four bullet wounds and he was treated in St. Augustine.

After residing in Charleston, S.C., Atlanta and visiting England he returned to Florida. He became friends with John Anderson (one of the partners who built the Hotel Ormond), John Andrew and Charles Bostrom. When the settlers of the New Britain colony decided to incorporate, in 1880, John Anderson and the Bostrom's suggested the change in name from "New Britain" to "Ormond". James and his wife Elizabeth came to spend their winters at Ormond for years afterwards and when the Hotel Ormond opened on January 1, 1888, James was an honored guest.

Dummett Plantation Ruins

The Dummett Plantation Ruins are located 2-miles north of the Tomoka State Park entrance on Old Dixie Highway. (On the right)

If you are traveling south on Old Dixie Highway from the Ormond Park, go 2.8 miles and the Dummett Plantation Ruins will be on your left.

A Public Place
(No Facilities)

Dummett Plantation Ruins.

A Guide to Walk, Bike and Drive Our History

Dummett Plantation Ruins

Colonel Thomas Henry Dummett was a planter and officer in the British Marines. He escaped an insurrection in Barbados by hiding in a sugar cask. He was loaded aboard one of his ships by slaves to sail away safely.

First settling in Connecticut, and then wanting a warmer climate, Colonel Dummett purchased two East Florida plantations containing 3000 acres, in 1825. After several failed attempts to grow sugarcane, Thomas brought in an expert from the West Indies and his sugarcane fields were soon large enough to support a sugar mill and rum distillery. The Dummett Plantation sugar mill became one of the first steam operated mills in the area.

Anna Dummett (daughter of Colonel Dummett) recollects a lavish lifestyle with log home, large yard, green Bermuda grass, and moss draped trees. The home had a big fireplace, brightly polished andirons, an old fashioned wine cooler of solid mahogany and bound with brass, claw footed tables, family portraits, and heavy silver on the buffet. This extravagant lifestyle ended when the Seminole War broke out and the Dummetts fled to St. Augustine. The plantation was destroyed by the Seminole Indians.

Anna reflects: "Every article of cloth had been taken, the house was full of feathers and hair from the beds, the leather torn from the furniture and books and almost every article of furniture broken. The family portraits had been taken from the walls and the eyes shot out by arrows......every article of china cut-glass was broken."

A family friend dug up the Dummett family silver that had been buried before the family abandoned the plantation. He put it aboard a boat and sailed it safely (through Indian fire) to St. Augustine.

In St. Augustine, the Dummetts rented one of the oldest houses in the town. Today this house (with changes) is known as the St. Francis Inn.

Nocoroco and Tomoka Basin

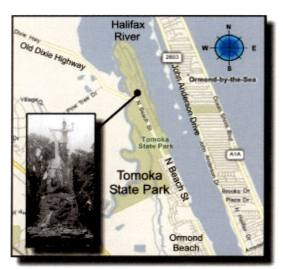

Located 2-1/2 miles north of Granada on North Beach Street. The Tomoka Basin is approximately 400 acres of shallow estuarine bay, located at the confluence of the Tomoka and Halifax Rivers.

A Public Park

    Nomadic bands of Indians entered Florida more than 14,000 years ago. The Timucuan Indians inhabited the area of the Tomoka Basin known as Nocoroco by the time the Europeans arrived. This location was documented by Alvaro Mexia in 1605.

A Guide to Walk, Bike and Drive Our History

Nocoroco and Tomoka Basin

The Timucuan spoke several dialects and consisted of various tribes. Their villages were fortified with a stockade and an entrance guardhouse. A community house, centrally located, served as the residence of the chief. Smaller huts surrounded that residence and housed the village families. The houses were circular and dome-shaped with palmetto thatched roofs and walls.

Chiefs and important officials tattooed their bodies with designs in red, blue and black. Strands of Spanish moss provided their body covering. A knot was used to tie the long hair of the men and that permitted them to carry arrows for hunting. The Timucuan Indians were skilled hunters, using bow, arrow, spear and snares. Varieties of animals and reptiles were part of their diet, including turtles, birds, and alligator. Plants, roots, nuts and berries added variety. Deer was an important meat source, and they were hunted by the Timucuan in a disguise using deer hide and head.

Living near both the Halifax and Tomoka rivers, natives used wooden dugout canoes for transportation and hunting. Many have been found preserved in the lakes and rivers. When an important Timucuan died, he or she was laid to rest in a sand burial mound and often buried with possessions.

Nocoroco and Tomoka Basin

Dix House

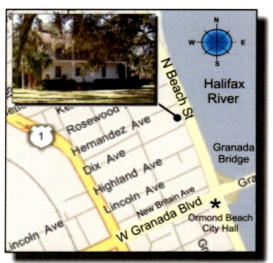

Located at 178 North Beach Street. From the NW base of the Granada Bridge, travel north on N Beach Street about three blocks and you will see the Dix House on the left. The Dix House is the second house past Dix Ave.

National Register of Historic Places

A Private Home

The Dix House - 178 North Beach Street.

Dix House was built for Eliza and Ruth Dix. When Eliza became ill before the house was completed, kind citizens of the New Britain colony (now Ormond Beach) came to help.

A Guide to Walk, Bike and Drive Our History

Dix House

The upper floor of Dix House was not divided into rooms, but left as a large room where the settlers met for parties, picnics, meetings and religious services. Celebrations were grand. Fish, venison, bear meat, turtle, oysters, wild turkey, cakes and pies would be served. Ladies wore sunbonnets and aprons and men homemade hats of palmetto leaves. Music filled the air and dancing went on into the night.

In March 1880, it was decided that the colony be incorporated and a new name be chosen. A notice was posted for 30 days in 3 public places within the New Britain Colony. Everyone in the colony was informed of a meeting for incorporation. On the 22nd day of April 1880, a majority of citizens met at "Dix Hall" and voted to change New Britain to Ormond in order to honor the family who owned Damietta Plantation prior to the Seminole War.

It was John A. Bostrom and John Anderson who proposed the new name. James Francis, a merchant of the colony from a prominent New Britain, Connecticut, family wished to retain the name New Britain. He offered a pound of sugar (a precious and scarce food item) to anyone who voted his way. The settlers voted for the change instead. A celebration ensued as men, women, and children marched holding home made banners and flags with improvised drum and horn music.

William McNary Home

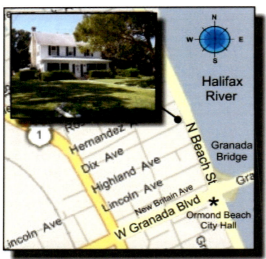

Located at 166 N. Beach Street. From the NW base of the Granada Bridge, travel north on N Beach Street about three blocks and you will see the McNary Home on the left at the NW corner of Dix Ave. and N Beach Street.

A Private Home

The William McNary Home - 166 N. Beach.

A Guide to Walk, Bike and Drive Our History

William McNary Home

Mr. William McNary fought in the Civil War on the Union Side, though his advanced age should have disqualified him. Cabinetmakers by trade, William and his son Charles, worked for Corbin Lock Co, New Britain, Connecticut, before moving to Florida in the 1870's and building one of the first houses on the mainland of the New Britain colony.

The home, a two story, white structure had an open front porch, which faced the Halifax River, and William McNary or "Grandpa" as he was known could often be seen reading and feeding peanuts to the squirrels.

At a meeting on April 22, 1880, the townspeople met to incorporate the town of New Britain and change to name to Ormond. Charles McNary was appointed to count the votes to change the name. Later Charles held positions including councilman, mayor, justice of the peace and secretary-treasurer of the Ormond Building & Loan Association. During his service to the Ormond City Council meeting, Charles and his fellow councilmen drew up ordinances specifying the duties of town marshal, clerk, treasurer, assessor and collector. When the Ormond City Council met at Charles McNary's house on May 8, 1880, James Francis was appointed to a committee of one to order the town seal. The design was to be a Banana Tree with the inscription "Ormond, Florida, Incorporated April 22nd, 1880" inserted in a circle. The "Banana Tree" symbol still exists as the centerpiece of the city seal of Ormond Beach.

Charles McNary had a large fruit grove that grew peach, pear, orange, nut, guava and persimmon. Unfortunately, freezes in 1886 and 1891 severely damaged his orange grove.

In later years, the lower front porch of the McNary house was enclosed and the upper porch removed.

Ormond Beach Historic Places

Ormond Yacht Club

Located at the foot of Lincoln Avenue, along the west bank of Halifax River. From the NW base of the Granada Bridge, travel north on N Beach Street a couple of blocks and you will see The Yacht club along the bank of the Halifax River.

A Private Club

Ormond Beach Yacht Club, 2006.

A Guide to Walk, Bike and Drive Our History

Ormond Yacht Club

In 1910, 40 residents of Ormond Beach decided they needed a place to moor their boats, so they arranged to have a 2 story building built on the west bank of the Halifax River.

The agreement with the City of Ormond was that the building would not appear on the tax rolls, so even today it does not appear on any Ormond Beach maps.

Architect Grove of Daytona submitted tentative plans for a 21' x 36' building with a 7' porch on the south and east sides. A long dock was to extend from the club-house to the river with a boat shed and stalls at the end.

Shortly after the building was completed a severe storm destroyed the dock and shed and it was never replaced. Activities included cards, reading, pool, dinners and dances.

In its heyday the club was a central part of the social activity of the community.

Present membership is about 25 men, all Ormond Beach residents. The second floor is no longer used. The lower level is used for cards and pool.

Anderson-Price Memorial Library
(Village Improvement Association
And Woman's Club)

42 N. Beach Street. From the NW base of the Granada Bridge, travel north on N Beach Street about one block and you will see the Anderson-Price Memorial Library Building on your left.

National Register of Historic Places

Owned by the Ormond Beach Historical Trust Inc. Since 2002

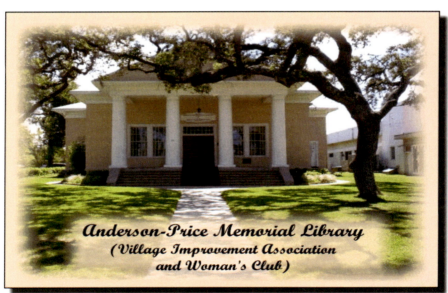

Anderson-Price Memorial Library Building Postcard, 2006

A Guide to Walk, Bike and Drive Our History

Anderson-Price Memorial Library (Village Improvement Association and Woman's Club)

Sixteen citizens met at the Ormond Union Church in January, 1891, to organize a Village Improvement Association. Originally, only men were permitted to become members and later membership was limited to women only! Dues were assessed at twenty-five cents. The mission of the club was "To promote neatness and order in the village; do whatever may tend to improve and beautify our town as a place of residence and keep it in a healthful condition". Mrs. Joseph Price was the first President.

Eventually the members of the V.I.A. purchased a building from John Brink in 1905 for a cost of $1,200, and a housekeeper was hired for three dollars per month. A few years later Mrs. Margaret Howe gave a house and lot to the club. The house and original VIA clubhouse were sold about 1912 and from these funds a new building was erected on Beach Street. It was named the Anderson-Price Memorial Library and Village Improvement Association building in appreciation of the assistance to the club by both John Anderson and Joseph Price.

In 1957 the Village Improvement Association was changed to the Ormond Beach Woman's Club and through a donation from a long time member, needed improvements were made including an addition (kitchen and pantry) in 1960.

In 1969, the Ormond Beach Regional Library was built on Beach Street. The Ormond Beach Woman's Club gave its books, but also added a $1000 gift for the purchase of books for the new library.

In 2002, ownership of the Anderson Price Memorial Library building was transferred to the Ormond Beach Historical Trust, under the leadership of J. Donald Bostrom – President of the Ormond Beach Historical Trust.

James Carnell Home

Located at 40 North Beach Street. From the NW base of the Granada Bridge, travel north on N Beach Street one short block and you will see the James Carnell Home on your left. It is now the Veranda Beauty Salon.

**Beauty Salon
Open to Public**

James Carnell Home - 40 North Beach Street.

James Carnell Home

James Carnell was born September 30, 1849 in Leicester, England. His family moved to Connecticut in the 1850s. When James Carnell reached adulthood, he became a mackerel fisherman. He and 2 companions were fishing off Nova Scotia and a fog caused them to go off course. For four days they drifted with no food or water and were finally rescued. One man died. The other 2 were exhausted with lips so swollen they could not speak. During his admittance to the hospital, Mr. Carnell was found to have contracted inflammatory rheumatism.

In 1875, he moved to Florida as a member of the New Britain settlement. When James Carnell moved to the New Britain colony he was on crutches. However, after six weeks in Florida, he put away the crutches and never used them again. He married in 1879 and had three sons. His wedding to Caroline Kitchell was the second to take place in the original colony which became the city of Ormond in 1880.

Carnell's first business in Ormond Beach was an orange grove which was destroyed in the freeze of 1895. He then organized the Carnell Jelly Factory that for 25 years produced guava jelly, citrus marmalades and preserved tropical fruits. He encouraged farmers to grow fruits, especially figs. He also operated a successful real estate business. When Mr. Carnell opened his prosperous preserve business, he produced 55 tons a year. He served on the City Council, Postmaster, Mayor and was a very active Mason. James Carnell was one of the original members of the Ormond Yacht Club.

James Carnell died in 1917. His Great Floridian plaque is located at the Veranda Beauty Salon (former Carnell House), 40 North Beach Street, Ormond Beach.

Pilgrim's Rest Primitive Baptist Church

Located at 1 North Beach Street., at the NW base of the Granada Bridge. There is public parking for about 15 cars in the adjacent parking lot.

A Public Building

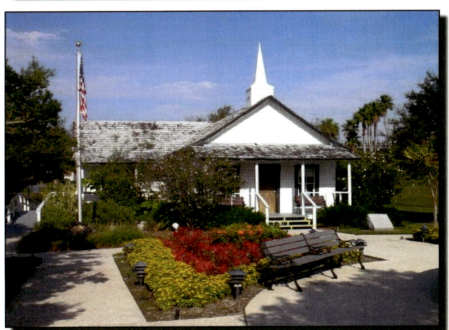

Pilgrim's Rest Primitive Baptist Church - 1 North Beach Street.

A Guide to Walk, Bike and Drive Our History

Pilgrim's Rest Primitive Baptist Church

In the 1800's, the development along Groover Creek and the Tomoka River, about 5 miles west of present day US1, became known as the Tomoka Settlement. The settlers built a frame building they named Pilgrim's Rest Baptist Church. Next to the church, a cemetery was also opened. However, in 1895, freezing temperatures destroyed the orange groves the settlers had planted, and since the settlement depended on the citrus for income, they decided to move closer to the Ormond Beach area where the groves were not as heavily affected.

Because the settlers tired of traveling to their church still located in the Tomoka Settlement, they decided in 1910, to move the one room church to a piece of land that was donated. Today, that land is located near Granada and Nova Rd. A new graveyard was also located nearby. Pilgrim's Rest Cemetery is still to be found at that location, and has more than 300 gravesites, including seven Confederate soldiers buried there. Meanwhile, in 1988, the land on which the church was located was sold and the church was due for demolition. However, many concerned citizens and local residents contributed to have the historic structure moved to city owned property. Today, the little church has been esthetically placed in a park at the foot of the Granada Bridge on the northwest corner.

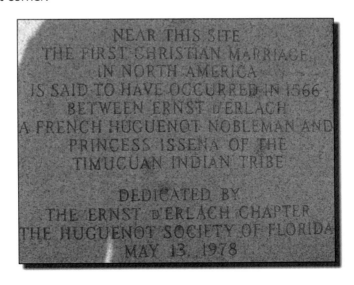

Lippincott Mansion (Melrose Hall)

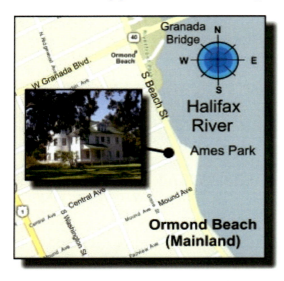

Located at 150 S. Beach Street. From the SW base of the Granada Bridge, turn south on S Beach Street and travel a few blocks along the Halifax River. The Lippincott Mansion is at the NW corner of Central Ave. and S Beach St., just across from Ames Park.

National Register of Historic Places

A Private Home

Lippincott Mansion (Melrose Hall) - 150 South Beach Street.

A Guide to Walk, Bike and Drive Our History

Lippincott Mansion (Melrose Hall)

Lippincott Mansion was built in 1895 with eclectic, Queen Anne elements. The house is 3 stories with shingle siding and a three story round room at the front which was used for social affairs.

This three-story 9,000 square foot mansion was built in 1895 for Anne Lippincott. She later sold it to her sister, Harriet. Its style is described as eclectic, combining elements of Queen Anne and Romanesque. It was later used as a residence and office, and after it was purchased by William Scobie in 1899, it was known as Melrose Hall. This was added to the National Register of Historic Places in 1985.

The Lippincott sisters owned and operated this home as a boarding house. This section of town was plated originally as "Melrose".

Lippincott Mansion (Melrose Hall) - 150 South Beach Street.

The Porches

176 S. Beach Street. From the SW base of the Granada Bridge, turn south on S Beach Street and travel a few blocks along the Halifax River. The Porches is at the SW corner of Central Ave. and South Beach St.

National Register of Historic Places

A Private Home

The Porches - 176 South Beach Street.

A Guide to Walk, Bike and Drive Our History

The Porches

This house is a 1883 frame vernacular building with porches on three sides. Bill Barker, a New York artist who came to Florida for his health, built it.

Bill Barker also built, in 1890, a home to the south of The Porches for his mother. The Stone House (Ames House) across the street (South Beach Street) was also built by Barker in 1910.

All three homes were eventually owned by Blanche Butler Ames and General Adelbert Ames for family use during the winter season.

The Porches - 176 South Beach Street.

"The Whim" at Ames Park and Ames House

Located at 173 South Beach Street

From the SW base of the Granada Bridge, turn south on S Beach Street and travel a few blocks along the Halifax River. The Ames House will be on the left. Ample public parking is available.

A Public Building

The Ames House - Ames Park - 173 South Beach Street.

A Guide to Walk, Bike and Drive Our History

"The Whim" at Ames Park
and
Ames House

Mrs. Blanche Butler Ames and husband General Adelbert Ames were prominent citizens of Ormond Beach. After their first home purchase, Mrs. Ames began collecting other houses for winter residences for her children and grandchildren. These included the Stone House, the Cedars, the Ship Cabin, the Porches, Melrose Hall, Cozy Nook, Orange Lodge, the Last Straw and the Shells.

Mrs. Ames was the beautiful daughter of Benjamin F. Butler, a representative in Congress from Massachusetts. Her husband was General Adelbert Ames, a graduate of West Point, brevetted Major General at the Battle of Bull Run, a senator from Mississippi and a recipient of the Congressional Medal of Honor.

After spending many winters in Ormond Beach at the Hotel Ormond, Mrs. Ames became bored. Her husband spent his days playing golf with John D. Rockefeller and so Mrs. Ames took her boredom into her own hands and began to take walks across the wooden bridge that spanned the Halifax River. These excursions led to the purchase of a two story fame (pinewood) house on the river. The home became known as The "Whim" and it was used for their winter stays in Ormond Beach.

Unfortunately, "The Whim" was torn down some years ago and Ames Park is now located on the site. Today, the large, gray, stone block house, built in 1910, immediately north of the park, once owned by the Ames family, still stands and is a public building occupied by the Ormond Beach City Attorney. Professor Oakes Ames, son-in-law of Blanche Butler Ames and General Adelbert Ames, was a famous expert on orchids, and used the property as a guesthouse.

Ormond Beach Historic Places

Ormond Indian Mound

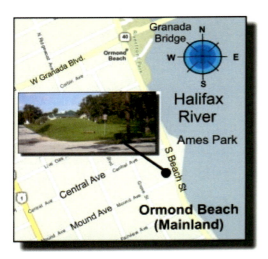

Located at the corner of Mound Avenue and South Beach Street. From the SW base of the Granada Bridge, travel south on S Beach Street until you see Ames Park on the left side of the road. The Ormond Indian Mound is located on the right at Mound Ave.

Open to Public

Ormond Indian Mound - at the corner of Mound Avenue and South Beach Street.

A Guide to Walk, Bike and Drive Our History

Ormond Indian Mound

The Ormond Indian burial mound is the finest and most intact burial site in eastern Florida and was constructed sometime after 800 A.D. The site contains over 100 people buried in the sand.

Also associated with the Ormond Mound was a Charnel House where the bodies were prepared for the afterlife. The dead were laid out on wooden racks and allowed to decompose. Afterwards, the bones were "bundled" and buried in mounds during special ceremonies. Such a structure was used by the St. Johns period Indians for removal of the deceased's flesh and drying of the bones. Bundles of bones were then buried in the mound during special ceremonies.

Community efforts came together to save the Ormond Beach site from destruction in 1982.

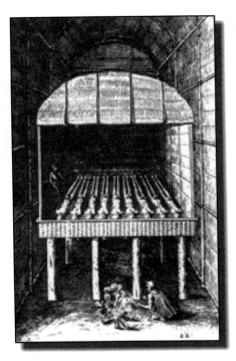

A charnel house, a structure used to store bodies prior to burial, was associated with the Ormond Mound. Charnel houses were used by St. Johns people to prepare the corpses of mostly high-ranking and important people for the afterlife. The dead were laid out on wooden racks and allowed to decompose. A charnel house attendant, usually a high priest, would carefully remove the flesh from the bones as they decayed. After the bodies dried away, the charnel house priest would end up with individual sets of cleaned bones. Each disarticulated set of bones was bundled up and buried in mounds during special ceremonies. This method accounts for the many skeletons found in burial mounds.

Rigby School

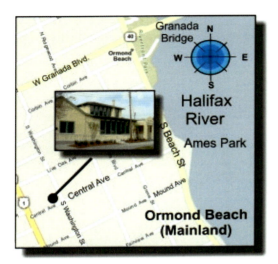

Located at the corner of Central Avenue and South Washington Street., Ormond Beach

Ormond Beach City Owned

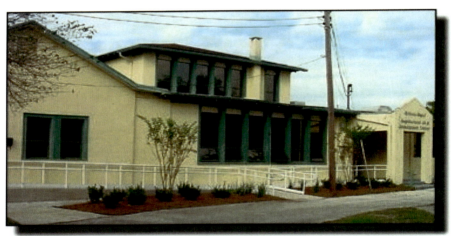

Rigby School - at the corner of Central Avenue and South Washington St

The Rigby School was founded in 1911 and originally called the Ormond Colored School at Yonge Street (US1 and Midway Avenue). In the 1920's the school exhibited Mediterranean or Mission influences in its design with exposed rafter ends and capped chimney caps. At some point, asphalt shingles replaced a clay roof.

A Guide to Walk, Bike and Drive Our History

Rigby School

The Rigby Elementary School (founded in 1911) was originally called Ormond Colored School and was located at the corner of South Yonge Street (US I) and Midway Avenue. Sanborn fire maps of 1921 confirm the former location of the school.

The school was subsequently moved to its present site on Central Avenue near South Yonge Street (US 1). The current stucco-over-frame structure was built in 1924 on what was then a five (5) acre tract. The structure originally consisted of seven small classrooms, a cafeteria, and a principal's office.

Ms. Lela Scott was one of the first graduates of the new school in 1924. Ms. Scott went on to be a teacher at the Ormond Colored School until the school closed in 1969 and Ms. Scott retired.

During the 1939/1940 school year, School Board information states that the Ormond Colored School was renamed for Major George N. Rigby, former mayor of Ormond Beach from 1916 through 1928. However, the 1931 Sanborn maps indicate the school was named in honor of Maude Lawrence Rigby. It is not readily known what relation Maude Lawrence Rigby was to former Mayor Rigby. The 1931 Sanborn maps, however, no longer refer to the school as a "colored" school.

In 1956, a one-story clay-tile building, containing two (2) classrooms, a band room and a music room, was added to the school campus. Rigby Elementary had grades 1 through 8 until 1962. From 1962 until it's closing in 1969, Rigby Elementary served grades 1-6. The closing of the school was a result of court-ordered integration in the 1969-70 school year and students were transferred to Ormond Elementary on Corbin Avenue.

The former Rigby School was deeded to the City of Ormond Beach in 1987 and was converted into the Ormond Beach Neighborhood Child Development Center.

Ormond Elementary School

Located at the corner of Corbin and Ridgewood Ave.

A Public Building

Ormond Beach Elementary School at the corner of Corbin and Ridgewood Ave.

A Guide to Walk, Bike and Drive Our History

Ormond Elementary School

The present school was originally called Corbin School and built in 1917.

Ormond's first school teacher was Jennie Bacon, wife of Chauncey Bacon (Number 9 Plantation owner). She taught 6 boys in a log cabin. Alice Lulu Foulke taught at the one room school located at Lincoln & Ridgewood.

J. Don Bostrom, grandson of John Andrew Bostrom, attended Ormond Elementary School and then Seabreeze High School on beachside. Many local residents have fond memories of their days attending school at Ormond Elementary School.

Ormond Beach Historic Places

The Three Chimneys

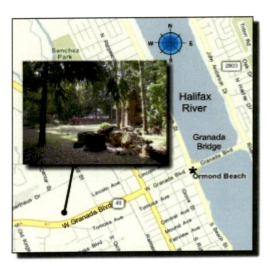

Located on West Granada Blvd. between Yonge Ave. and Nova Road on the north side, just west of the Moose Family Center.

A State Property, Managed by the Ormond Beach Historical Trust Inc.

Phone 386 677 7005 for information

The Three Chimneys Sugar Mill Ruins.

A Guide to Walk, Bike and Drive Our History

The Three Chimneys is the oldest sugar mill and rum distillery in North America. Richard Oswald, a wealthy Scotsman, received in 1764 a 20,000-acre grant from King George II to cultivate 5-plantations, raise sugar cane, and produce sugar and rum. America's first rum was produced at the Three Chimneys distillery, originally known as the Swamp Settlement.

Although he was an absentee owner, Oswald ordered the land cleared, canals built and ditches dug by 50 slaves in order to plant sugar cane and crops. Samuel Huey was the overseer and the slaves cleared 300 acres. Huey drank to excess and mistreated the slaves and consequently, they drowned him.

Successful plantation development at the other four plantations was thwarted by a severe freeze and poor growing conditions. He turned to indigo and rice as his main cash crops. Finally, the Swamp Settlement's sugar cane fields flourished and America's first rum was produced under the oaks of The Three Chimneys.

In 1769 Oswald added 70 more slaves, mostly women, to begin a Negro nursery that grew to 240 by 1780. The Three Chimneys was purchased by the State of Florida in 2003 to preserve the ruins and encompass 40 acres for a park. In May of 2003 the Ormond Beach Historical Trust was awarded a 50-year lease to maintain and improve the site.

The 3-Chimneys as it appeared prior to 2003.

Ormond Beach Historic Places

A Guide to Walk, Bike and Drive Our History

Halifax Country Timeline

Period	Year	Place	Event	Description
20,000 BC	Years Ago	Florida	Silver Bluff Terrace	Daytona Beach is located on the Silver Bluff Terrace, an ancient ocean bottom that was formed during the last Glacial Period, approximately 20,000 years ago. Ground sloth's, rearing approximately twelve feet high, once roamed our forests along-side saber-toothed tigers, mammoths, mastodons, giant armadillos, camels, prehistoric horses and the like.
12,000 BC to 15,000 BC		Florida		Following food supplies, mainly roaming herds of large mammals such as mastodons and mammoths, the Asians migrated over the land bridge and throughout the Americas, eventually finding their way into Florida some 15,000 years ago. Many archaeologists believe these early Floridians; called Paleo-Indians populated our coastal regions, now underwater because ancient coastlines were miles away from where they are today.
12,000 BC	Years Ago	Florida	First man came to Florida	These descendants of primitive Asiatics who migrated over the land bridge came to be called Indians. They hunted the animals along the Halifax and Tomoka Rivers, leaving burial mounds behind.
7000 BC		Florida	Early Archaic Period	After 7,000 BC, the Earth's climate began to change as a warming trend caused glaciers to melt and release tremendous amounts of water into our oceans. This was the end to the last great Ice Age and the beginning Archaic period where hunters and gathers began to expand out of the central highlands of Florida.
5000 BC		Florida	Middle Archaic Period	As ancient Indian populations grew near present-day cities of Ocala and Gainesville the prehistoric

				peoples migrated into areas along the St. Johns river where they found an abundance of fish, game and freshwater shellfish, mainly snail and mussel.
4000 BC		Volusia	Mount Taylor Period	The Archaic populations are known archaeologically as the Mount Taylor culture, named after the Mount Taylor site, a freshwater shell mound on the St. Johns river in Volusia County.
2000 BC		Volusia	Late Archaic Period	The Archaic tradition, or the way Archaic people lived, continued for thousands of years. Around 2000 BC, the Archaic people of Volusia County acquired pottery-making technology, from outside cultures. Volusia County contains several sites along the St. Johns river, which have produced some of the oldest pottery in North America.
1000 BC		Volusia East Coast	Transitional	Orange fiber-tempered pottery recovered from the Tomoka Stone and Cotton sites indicate that prehistoric peoples were using these areas about 1,500 BC. Evidence from the lower Tomoka River Basin on Ormond Beach indicates that Late Archaic peoples were living along the coasts of Volusia County year-round rather than at certain times of the year.
500 BC		Volusia	Early St. Johns (St Johns I)	The end of the Transitional Period (Orange Period) is marked by changes in pottery types resulting from the use of different tempering materials such as sand, which was used along with or in place of plant fibers. By 500 BC, Orange pottery was replaced by a chalky ware known by archaeologists as St. Johns. The St. Johns people occupied two major regions in Volusia County – the St John's River basin to the west and the environmentally rich estuaries of the Halifax and Indian Rivers on the

A Guide to Walk, Bike and Drive Our History

				east coast.
1500's	Early	Volusia	Timucuan Indians occupied this area.	The Timucuan Tribe was one of main tribes occupying Florida when Spaniards made their first visit. The tribes lived in fortified villages along Tomoka and Halifax Rivers.
1513		Ponce Inlet		Ponce De Leon explores Ponce Inlet area
1500's	Late	Volusia	Timucuan Indians primary settlement called "Nocoroco"	The primary Timucuan settlement was called "Nocoroco" and is thought to have been located where Tomoka State Park is today. Spanish captain DePrado documented this village in the late 1500's in writings to the King of Spain. DePrado also documented the declining welfare of this tribe
1565		St Augustine		Spanish establish St. Augustine, and gain control of Florida, driving out the French.
1566		Volusia	First Christian marriage in North America	First Christian marriage in North America at present day site, Bailey River Bridge Gardens (c.1566) A French Huguenot, Ernst d'Erlach, wed Princess Issena of the Timucuan Indian Tribe.
1600's	Early	Florida East Coast	Alvaro Mexia explores Florida's northeast coast	In the early 1600's Alvaro Mexia was sent on an exploring expedition down Florida's northeast coast and created a map showing Nocoroco on a peninsula between two rivers.
1700's		Florida East Coast	Area population grew as many settlers turned to plantation development	British landowners came in the 1700's and had rice and indigo plantations. Later, planters from the Bahamas developed plantations into a "Sugar Empire." These plantations were destroyed in the Second Seminole Indian War. (1831 - 1842)
1700's	Mid	Florida East coast	Florida's first highway, the King's Road, was constructed	While under British occupation, Florida's first highway, the King's Road, was constructed. It covered 106 miles from St. Augustine to New Smyrna Beach and 48 miles from Palatka to Amelia Island. It was

Ormond Beach Historic Places

				begun in 1771 and completed in 1775.
1763		Florida Territory	Spain ceded Florida to England	Spain ceded Florida to England after the Seven Years War. Soon after, settlers began arriving in the Halifax Country area.
1763		Turnbull Plantation		Turnbull Plantation deserted by indentured settlers who go to St. Augustine.
1764	July 24	Ormond	Scotsman Richard Oswald receives 20,000 acre land grant	With 50 slaves, Oswald launched his first settlement in a Native American-inhabited subtropical region of coastal Florida.
1765		Ormond	The nations first sugar mill and rum distillery begun. Later to be called, The Three Chimneys	The Three Chimneys site contains the ruins of the first sugar mill and rum distillery in North America. It dates back to 1765 when Scotsman named Richard Oswald established a sugar cane plantation on a 20,000-acre land grant. In 1765 fifty slaves and an overseer by the name of Samuel Huey walked from St. Augustine to what is now Ormond Beach. They cleared 300 acres, planted sugarcane, and built and operated the first sugar mill and rum distillery.
1766		Ormond	British government grants 20,000 acres to Richard Oswald	The British government gave many land grants to its subjects, including 20,000 acres to Richard Oswald in 1766. Mount Oswald was a rice and indigo plantation encompassing what is now Tomoka State Park.
1768		New Smyrna	Turnbull Settlement Begins	Dr. Turnbull settles a group of Greeks, Italians and Minorcans in the largest British colonial attempt in North America at New Smyrna.
1785		Ormond	British left Florida	When the British left in 1785, the meager beginnings of a plantation capital fell into ruin and did not flourish again until the Spanish land grants of the early 1800's brought planters from the Bahamas.
1790				Spain attempts to settle outlands

A Guide to Walk, Bike and Drive Our History

				from St. Augustine, by use of land grants.
1700's	Late	Ormond	Timucuans entirely disappeared from the east coast of Florida	Within 200 years after DePrado's expedition, the Timucuans entirely disappeared from the east coast of Florida. It is thought their susceptibility to diseases brought by the Spaniards, emigration, raids from the Yamassee Indians, and the British raids from North Carolina sped their demise.
1783 to 1821		Florida	Second Spanish Period - Florida was ceded back to Spain in 1783	Spain was in possession of Florida from 1783 to 1821, when it became a United States Territory.
1803		Ponce Inlet		Antonio Pons (Ponz or Ponce), a New Smyrna Minorcan, is granted 175 acres on the point where the lighthouse now stands, which he had been farming for 20 years.
1806		Ponce Inlet		Antonio Pons is driven off by the Indians and moves to St. Augustine.
1812		Ponce Inlet		Antonio Pons is killed while serving the King of Spain during the Patriots War, started by the Americans.
1817		Florida	The first Seminole Indian war	While the United States was fighting the War of 1812 with Britain, a series of violent incidents aggravated hostility between the U.S. and the Seminole.
1817	April 18	Pre-Daytona	3200 acres grant made	The Samuel Williams land grant made by Governor Jose Coppinger.
1818		Florida	Spain ceded Florida to America	Floridians were paid $5 Million by Washington for their many claims against Spain.
1820		Ponce Inlet		Pons' widow receives an additional grant of 230 acres in return for her husband's service to Spain.

Ormond Beach Historic Places

1820		Ormond	James Ormond II returned to Damietta	James Ormond II returned to Damietta with his wife and four children, including James Ormond III in 1820.
1821		Florida	Florida becomes United States Territory	Spain was in possession of Florida from 1783 to 1821 when it became a United States Territory.
1821		Ponce Inlet	Live oak lumbering began	Florida ceded to United States by Spain. Live oak lumbering began at Los Mosquitoes (Ponce de Leon Inlet).
1829		Ormond	James Ormond II dies	When James Ormond II died in 1829, his family abandoned Damietta. He is buried about four miles north of Tomoka State Park. James Ormond III would return many years later.
1834		Ponce Inlet	New Smyrna destroyed by fire	First lighthouse built on New Smyrna side of Inlet was destroyed by Indians and a storm.
1835 to 1842		Florida	Second Seminole Indian war period	The second Seminole Indian War erupted in 1835. The battle was about hunting and fishing grounds and the freedom of movement of the Indians. There was a tremendous uprising against the planters and a massive evacuation to St. Augustine took place. The plantations soon fell victim to fiery raids.
1836		Ormond	Seminoles destroy Bulow Ville	John Joachim Bulow inherited the plantation from Charles Bulow, which was subsequently ravished by the Seminole Indians.
1842				Bartola Pacetti, descendant of an Italian settler at New Smyrna builds a house of driftwood on fifty acres of Turnbull Grant of the north side of the Inlet.
1854		Volusia County	Volusia County formed	After Florida entered the Union and Volusia County was created in 1854, there were some 20 families living in the entire county.
1855-1858		Florida	Third Seminole Indian war period	This struggle, also known as the Billy Bowlegs War, was the final clash of an intermittent guerilla conflict

A Guide to Walk, Bike and Drive Our History

				between the Seminole Indians of Florida and the United States. It had started in 1817 with fierce Seminole resistance to land-coveting white settlers encroaching from neighboring Georgia, and then resumed in 1835.
1860		Ponce Inlet	Ponce Inlet Purchased	Mercedes Pacetti gains Ponce Inlet Grant from heirs through a tax sale.
1861	Jan 9	New Britain	Village Improvement Association (VIA) formed.	Sixteen citizens met at the Ormond Union Church to organize a Village Improvement Association, later to become the Woman's Club
1868		New Britain	John Andrew Bostrom	John Andrew Bostrom and his brother Charles settled on the banks of the Halifax river.
1870		Ponce Inlet		Congress appropriates $60,000 to secure a site and build a lighthouse.
1870	Fall	Daytona		Mathias Day purchased 3200 acres from Christina Relf, sister to Samuel H Williams
1870/ 1871		Daytona		First land cleared in Daytona settlement to build a saw mill on Beach Street between Cedar and South Streets.
1871		Daytona		Mathias Day built the Colony House to be used while new colonists built their permanent residence.
1873		Ormond Beach	Phillip Corbin - locates 630-acre retirement tract of land	With the help of Andrew Bostrom, land-scouting trio locates suitable tract for retirement community, later purchased by Philip Corbin.
1874/ 1875		Ormond Beach	New Britain Colony formed	Philip Corbin purchased the Henry Yonge and Hernandez grants on the west banks of the Halifax River. The New Britain settlement was formed.
1876		U.S.	National elections ballot box seizer plot averted	The purported plot to seize presidential election ballot box and remove all Republican votes was foiled by sending a second courier with the actual ballot box.
1880	April 22	Ormond Beach	New Britain citizens met at	Other early pioneers brought by the Corbin Lock Company included

Ormond Beach Historic Places

			the Dix sisters home to decide if the town should be incorporated	the McNary family and the Dix sisters. These two families were highly involved in the early politics of New Britain. John Anderson and John Andrew Bostrom convincingly swayed the colony to name it Ormond in honor of the James Ormond family.
1882		Halifax Country	Bucks Stage Coach and Mail Line established	Buck's Stage route was established about 1882 from St. Augustine to Ormond and Daytona, via the Kings Road three times a week.
1883		Ponce Inlet	Lighthouse site purchased	Ten acres purchased from Bartola Pacetti for $400 for lighthouse reservation site.
1884		Ponce Inlet	Lighthouse engineer drowns in the Inlet	Major (formerly Brigadier General) Orville Babcock, appointed engineer for building the lighthouse and who named the community Ponce (Pons) Park, drowns in the Inlet.
1885		Volusia County	First two railroads begun	The first two railroads to enter Volusia County were started in Volusia County. They were the St Johns & Halifax River Railroad and the Jacksonville & Key West Railroad.
1886		Ormond Beach	First railroad arrives	The St Johns & Halifax River Railroad reach Ormond Beach.
1887	Nov 1	Ponce Inlet	Lighthouse goes into service	Lighthouse goes into service on November 1st of this year.
1888	Jan 1	Ormond Beach	Hotel Ormond Opens	Built in 1887 by John Anderson and Joseph Price, opened on January 1, 1888, the Hotel Ormond became one of the best-known hotels in the world.
1890		Ponce Inlet	La Ponce Hotel	Nathaniel Hasty files Ponce Park subdivision plat. La Ponce Hotel built on the river shore.
1891		Ormond Beach	Ormond Beach Woman's Club formed	"Aunt Nell" Pinkerton formed the village Woman's Club to help "Clean up"/beautify the village. They occupied a small house on Lincoln Ave., also used as the village library, Ormond's first.

A Guide to Walk, Bike and Drive Our History

1893		Ormond Beach	Ormond Beach Woman's Club expands	In 1893 a cottage on Lincoln Avenue was rented for $100 per year. The largest room in the cottage was to be used for a free public library and reading room, and the other rooms for committee meetings and a kitchen. Guests at the Ormond and Coquina Hotels donated many of the books and periodicals for the library.
1894		Ormond Beach	Woman's Club buys building on Halifax River	The Association bought a building on a large oak-covered lot facing the Halifax river for $1200.00
1895		Ormond Beach	Woman's Club joins the General Federation of Woman's Clubs	Members paid annual dues of 25 cents and held fund raising events on front lawn.
1903		Ormond Beach	Birthplace of Speed	John Anderson arranges the first automobile races on the hardened sands of Ormond Beach.
1903		Ormond Beach	Ormond Garage Built	Henry Flagler built the Ormond Garage "Gasoline Alley" for the preparation, testing and servicing of some of the most famous racing cars of the world.
1911		Ormond Beach	John Anderson 1838 - 1911	Dies in 1911, only a few months apart from his long-time friend and partner Joseph Price. An influential Ormond Beach pioneer.
1911		Ormond Beach	Joseph Price 1853 - 1911	Dies in 1911, only a few months apart from his long-time friend and partner John Anderson. An influential Ormond Beach pioneer.
1916		Ormond Beach	Woman's Club builds new clubhouse/ library	By 1916, the Woman's Club earned enough money to build the present clubhouse, The Anderson-Price Memorial Library Building.
1918		Ormond Beach	The Casements	John D. Rockefeller purchased the original three-story, 13-bedroom mansion in 1918 when the Huntington's put it on the market after becoming disenchanted with Florida.

Ormond Beach Historic Places

1949		Ormond Beach	Ormond Beach	City of Ormond becomes Ormond Beach.
1965		Ormond Beach	Ormond Beach Municipal Library planned	Woman's Club members convinced the city fathers to build a municipal library. Woman's Club donated their library books and $1000 for new books.
1969		Ormond Beach	Ormond Beach Municipal Library	Ormond Beach Municipal Library opens and is stocked with donated library books from the Woman's Club plus $1000 for new books.
1970's		Ormond Beach	The Casements is gutted by fire	Twice burned, The Casements stands vacant and is gutted.
1970		Ormond Beach	Ormond Garage placed on National Register of Historic Places	Ormond Garage placed on National Register of Historic Places by the U.S. Department of the Interior.
1972		Ormond Beach	The Casements is burned	Fire destroyed two rooms on the top floor and severely damaged others.
1973		Ormond Beach	The Casements purchased by city	The Casements is purchased by the city of Ormond Beach for $500,000.
1974		Ormond Beach	The Casements practically destroyed by vandals	Vandal induced fires practically destroyed any chances of the home being restored to its former elegance. Fortunately, an outpouring of public support and the city timely response finally rescued The Casements.
1976	Jan 7	Ormond Beach	Ormond Garage burns to ground	The 72-year old Ormond Garage is totally consumed by fire.
1977		Ormond Beach	City receives $449,000 Federal grant for The Casements restoration project	A Federal grant for $449,000 enables restoration on The Casements to begin.
1978		Ormond Beach	Hotel Ormond purchased	Peter L. Francis purchased the Hotel Ormond.
1979	Oct 1	Ormond Beach	The Casements opens to the public	On Oct 7, 1979, this delightful period home was opened to the public and serves as a cultural library and civic center for the city.

A Guide to Walk, Bike and Drive Our History

1980	July 11	Ormond Beach	Hotel Ormond listed on National Register of Historic Places	Hotel Ormond listed on National Register of Historic Places by the Department of the Interior
1983		Ormond Beach	Hotel Ormond purchased	Updesh Singh Cheema purchased the Hotel Ormond for $2.5 million.
1984		Ormond Beach	Hotel Ormond purchased	Ormond Partners Ltd. purchased the hotel for $3,605,000.
1984		Ormond Beach	Anderson-Price Memorial Building placed on National Register of Historic Places	Anderson-Price Memorial Library Building placed on National Register of Historic Places by the U.S. Department of the Interior. Building - #84000967
1986	Oct 16	Ormond Beach	City orders Hotel Ormond closed	City orders Hotel Ormond closed for fire and safety violations. The Hotel Ormond was vacated and its 79 elderly residents were forced to find new living facilities.
1987	March 12	Ormond Beach	Hotel Ormond and contents sold	Milton Pepper, Ormond Beach developer and businessman, purchased the Hotel Ormond at auction for $2,010,000.
1990		Ormond Beach	Ormond Beach Fire Chief proclaimed Hotel Ormond a fire hazard	The Fire Chief advised the City to either find an investor to restore the hotel or demolish it.
1991		Ormond Beach	Largest Wooden frame structure	Before it was demolished in 1992, the vast Hotel Ormond was considered to be the largest all-wooden frame structure in America still standing
1992		Ormond Beach	All plans to save the Hotel Ormond failed	All plans to save the Hotel Ormond failed
1992		Ormond Beach	Hotel Ormond Demolished	The Hotel Ormond met the jaws of the backhoe and was demolished
1995		Ormond Beach	Ormond Beach Historical Trust sets sights on The Three Chimneys ruins restoration	The Trust completed an archaeological survey on the site in 1995, secured a $20,000 grant for the Preservation Plan, which was published July 7, 1999, and successfully petitioned the state to

Ormond Beach Historic Places

			project	purchase 40 contiguous acres for a park.
1997		Ormond Beach	City opens Fortunato Park	Fortunato park opens with the restored Hotel Ormond cupola as its centerpiece.
2002		Ormond Beach	Anderson - Price Memorial Building deeded	The Ormond Beach Woman's Club deeded the Anderson-Price Memorial Building to the Ormond Beach Historical Trust Inc.
2003	May 29	Ormond Beach	State purchases Three Chimneys property	The State purchases the Three Chimneys property and the Ormond Beach Historical Trust was granted a 50-year lease to manage the site on Granada Blvd.

A Guide to Walk, Bike and Drive Our History

A Brief Bibliography of Florida History

All titles are available at the State Library of Florida and locally through the Ormond Beach Public Library.

Contact your local public library to borrow these and other titles on Florida's history. If titles are not available, items may be borrowed from the State Library through the interlibrary loan system.

Florida Photographic Collection. In accordance with the provisions of Section 257.35(6), Florida Statutes, "Any use or reproduction of material deposited with the Florida Photographic Collection shall be allowed pursuant to the provisions of paragraph (1)(b) and subsection (4), *provided that appropriate credit for its use is given.*"

Florida Cowman: A history of Florida cattle raising by Joe A. Akerman (Jimbob Printing Inc., 1989).

Florida's Past: People and events that shaped the state, V. 1, 2, 3 by Gene M. Burnett (Pineapple Press, c1988). Readable and informative essays on Florida history.

Florida: A short history by Michael V. Gannon (University Press of Florida, c1993).
A compact (168 pp.) history using the oldest records and physical remains of Europe and America. Compiled using the latest in technology and space to encapsulate the story of Florida.

The New History of Florida: by Michael V. Gannon (University Press of Florida, c 1996).
Twenty-two noted historians and anthropologists contributed to this work, the first comprehensive history of the state in 25 years. Writing for both lay and scholarly audiences, the authors present not only political, economic, military, and religious information but also social history and personal experiences.

Apalachee: The land between the rivers by John H. Hann (University Presses of Florida: University of Florida Press/Florida State Museum, c1988).
The focus in this work is on the Apalachee Indians and their interactions with the Spanish during the historic period.

Ormond Beach Historic Places

History of the Second Seminole War, 1835-1842: by John K. Mahon (University Presses of Florida, 1991, c1967). Sets the Second Seminole War in its broad historical context and demonstrates the close connection between the coming of this Indian war and the general issue of Negro slavery.

Indian mounds of the Atlantic coast: A guide to sites from Maine to Florida by Jerry N. McDonald (McDonald & Woodward Publishing Company, c1987). A guide to the extant publicly accessible mounds, earthworks, shell middens, stone structures, and other artificial landscape features built by American Indians in the Atlantic Coast Region of the U.S.

Archaeology of Precolumbian Florida: by Jerald T. Milanich (University Press of Florida, c1994). This record of Precolumbian Florida brings to life the 12,000- year story of the Native American Indians who lived in the state. Describes the indigenous cultures and explains why they developed as they did. Richly illustrated.

Florida Indians and the Invasion from Europe: by Jerald T. Milanich (University Press of Florida (1995)). Focusing on the native peoples of Florida and their interactions with Spanish and French explorers and colonists, the author describes the massive cultural change that transpired as a result of these contacts.

Yesterday's Florida: by Nixon Smiley (E.A. Seemann Publishers (1974)). Over 500 historic photographs, many of them never published before, record visually the heritage that history has bestowed on today's Floridians, natives or recent arrivals alike.

A History of Florida: by Charlton W. Tebeau (University of Miami Press, 1980).
Florida, its history and people, panoramically portrayed in an illuminating text and over 100 photographs, maps, and drawings.

Climb A Tree and Holler: by J. Donald Bostrom (Self Published, 1997). Remembering my Grandfather and stories about growing up in Ormond Beach, Florida.

Ormond-On-The-Halifax: by Alice Strickland (The Ormond Beach Historical Trust, Inc. 1980) A Centennial History of Ormond Beach, Florida.

A Guide to Walk, Bike and Drive Our History

Ormond's Historic Homes: by Alice Strickland (The Ormond Beach Historical Trust, Inc. 1992) From Palmetto-Thatched Shacks to Millionaire's Mansions.

True Natives – The Prehistory of Volusia County: by Dana Ste. Claire (Museum of Arts and Sciences Daytona Beach, Florida 1992). A brief yet detailed work is the end result of three years of research and fieldwork by the author, Dana Ste. Claire.

Our Place in History – Ormond Beach, Florida: by Ronald L. Howell (Halifax Country Publishers, Aug 1, 2006). A compilation of Ormond Beach, Florida history presented in pictorial and timeline format providing the reader with 16th through 19th century history. This book represents the Wall of History, created by J. Donald Bostrom for the Ormond Beach Historical Trust during his presidency.

History of Volusia County, Florida 1927: by Pleasant Daniel Gold (E.O. Painter Printing Company (1927)). In writing the history of Volusia County the aim has been to present simply a true chronology of events from earliest explorations to present time.

Historic Properties Survey of Daytona Beach, Florida: by Historic Property Associates, Inc. St Augustine, Florida, 1986. This project was initialized by the city of Ormond Beach and sponsored by the Ormond Beach Historical Trust to provide a concise documented history of Ormond Beach as of 1986.

Our Place in History – Ormond Beach, Florida – Front Cover

A Guide to Walk, Bike and Drive Our History

Our Place in History – Ormond Beach, Florida – Back Cover

Ormond Beach Historic Places

A Guide to Walk, Bike and Drive Our History

About the Authors

Ron and Alice Howell have been married since 1978 and have shared many dreams, experiences and adventures as they traveled around the world. This book is one of those "Dream Come True" events that has been nurtured over the past decade and made possible through their shared interest in knowing the history surrounding their home environment, Halifax Country.

Volusia County has been our home since the early 1970's and we have sought out many events in both east and west Volusia as progress has both enriched and disregarded our historical past. We have watched and participated in activities bringing such structures as DeBary Hall back from near ruin. We have attended art festivals on the wooden verandas of the grand Hotel Ormond, before its demolition in 1992.

These treasured experiences have kindled a desire to help, in our own way, preserve the history of Ormond Beach and surrounding communities belonging to our Halifax Country.

Ron is the author of the recently released book "Our Place in History – Ormond Beach, Florida". Ron also brings technology to this project as he uses his software development and technical engineering skills to help create this inspired book. Recent activities include web site design and development as well as design and production of many history related products. All graphics in this book were designed and produced by Ron.

Alice brings many years of educational and travel industry experience to this project. In recent years Alice has volunteered many hours to the Museum of Arts and Sciences, as a docent, providing museum tour and classroom experiences for children and adults alike. Later as staff, in the Education Department, Alice was instrumental in developing educational programs and facilitated children and adults through several major exhibits such as the Great Asian Dinosaur and the Glories of Ancient Egypt exhibits. Alice also provided character reenactment programs for the Museum.

Ormond Beach Historic Places

Order books, postcards and magnetic-bookmarks at
http://www.halifaxcountry.com

Be sure to inquire about large quantity discount pricing…